The Arts and Crafts COMPUTER

USING YOUR COMPUTER

AS AN ARTIST'S TOOL

Janet Ashford

Peachpit Press
BERKELEY, CALIFORNIA

THE ARTS AND CRAFTS COMPUTER:
Using Your Computer as an Artist's Tool
Janet Ashford

Peachpit Press
1249 Eighth Street
Berkeley, CA 94710
(800) 283-9444, (510) 524-2178
(510) 524-2221 (fax)

Find us on the World Wide Web at: www.peachpit.com
To report errors, please send a note to errata@peachpit.com
Peachpit Press is a division of Pearson Education

ISBN 0-201-73482-6

0 9 8 7 6 5 4 3 2 1

Printed and bound in the United States of America.

♻ Printed on 100# Resolve Matte Recycled

Acknowledgments

MY FAMILY HELPS ME in many ways. I thank my brother Doug Isaacs, of Adage Graphics in Los Angeles, for helping me to upgrade my computer, for providing lots of computer-related tips drawn from his service bureau work and for being a good and loving brother. Thanks to my son, Rufus Ashford, for letting me reprint some of his art work. Thanks to my daughter, Florence Jean Ashford, for sharing her college design books and for letting me reproduce some of her work. It's a pleasure to watch as she studies typography, illustration and design and learns these fundamentals from the ground up. Thanks to my daughter, Molly Ashford, for letting me use her as a photographic model and also for her companionable presence and many good critiques in the studio as I worked on the projects for this book. Finally, many thanks to my sweetheart Tom Logan for being a patient, tolerant and generous member of the household.

MANY FRIENDS AND COLLEAGUES have helped me develop the ideas for this book. I especially want to thank Genie Shenk for introducing me to book arts through her wonderful classes at the Athenaeum Library of Music and Arts in La Jolla, California. Also I thank Marylee Bytheriver and Chris Rolik, who taught me a great deal in their book arts classes at the Mendocino Art Center. Thanks to Marge Stewart, Jima Abbott and the rest of the staff at the Mendocino Art Center for their support of my computer graphics classes and to all my students there, who teach me by the questions they ask. Thanks to Janet Martini for permission to reproduce some of her artist books and for her enthusiastic interest in my book idea. Thanks to the staff and supporters of the Mendocino Community Library, a private lending library with many resources on the arts. Thanks also to Catherine Fishel, editor of *Dynamic Graphics* magazine, for many great "crafty" ideas. Thanks to Jim Heid and Bob Laughton of the "Point and Click" computer radio show on KZYX, community-sponsored radio for Mendocino County. Thanks for Christine Schomer and P.S. Mueller for permission to reproduce their kite and cartoon, respectively. Finally, thanks to John Odam and Linnea Dayton, my co-authors on previous graphics books, for their continuing friendship and inspiration.

THE PEOPLE AT PEACHPIT PRESS have been flexible and supportive with all four of the books I've done with them. Thanks to Nancy Ruenzel, publisher, for her enthusiastic support of this book and to Victor Gavenda for his gracious presence as my editor. Thanks to Lisa Brazieal for her careful production work, to Gary-Paul Prince for his adroit marketing and to Janet Villanueva for finding recycled paper on which to print this book.

MANY THANKS to the publishers who sent review copies of their books, including Lark Books, Peachpit Press, NAPP Publishers, New Riders, Rockport Publishers and Stemmer House. Thanks to the companies that sent samples of their digital media and products including Create-A-Pad, Direct Imagination, Micro Format (special thanks to Steve Singer), Mirage Inkjet Technology and RoyalBrites. Finally, thanks to the companies that sent samples of their arts and crafts products, including The C-Thru Ruler Company, Flax Art & Design (special thanks to Howard Flax), RoyalBrites and Xyron.

Contents

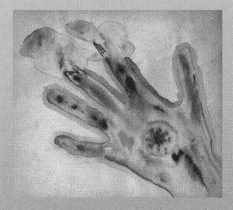
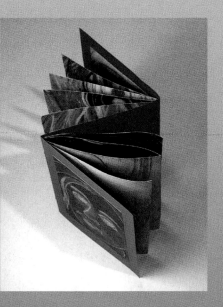

Introduction

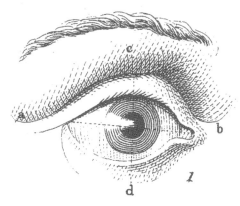

 FEW YEARS AGO I was asked to write an article about illustrators who began their careers with traditional art materials and later switched to computer graphics. None regretted the change, but most missed working with their hands. They felt a need for *touch* in their art and tried to keep working with traditional media in their spare time.

I feel the same way. I started out drawing and painting with "real" pencils and brushes, before the days of the personal computer. But I also did writing and publishing, so the first time I saw PageMaker running on a Mac Plus in 1986, I knew it would transform the way I worked. When Illustrator, FreeHand and Photoshop came along I was really hooked. It became possible to write, edit, design and illustrate an entire publication on the computer! These powerful tools changed my life and made it possible for me to earn a living at home, doing work I enjoy. I started writing "how-to" articles for magazines and eventually wrote six books on computer graphics. The most recent, written with John Odam, is *Start with a Scan: A Guide to Transforming Scanned Photos and Objects into High-Quality Art*, Second Edition, published by Peachpit Press in 2000. Based on what I learned from illustrators over the years, it includes information on how to turn a scan of almost anything into an attractive illustration. The many tips and techniques make *Start with a Scan* a great supplement to *The Arts and Crafts Computer*.

But after fifteen years of intense computer work, I feel the pull back to traditional art materials. I want to draw with pencils, paint with watercolors, cut with scissors and paste with glue. That's how the idea for this book was born. I was especially inspired by the first class I took in book arts, taught by artist Genie Shenk at the Athenæum Library of Music and Art in La Jolla, California. I greatly enjoyed the folding and stitching involved with bookbinding. But I also realized that my computer—combined with my scanner, laser printer and inkjet printer—were the perfect tools for creating some of the art I wanted for my projects and for printing multiple copies of it. So I set out to create *The Arts and Crafts Computer* to show readers how to have the best of both worlds—digital tools for creating and printing graphic images, combined with the tactile, three-dimensional and handmade qualities of the traditional arts and paper crafts.

When I began, I was thinking primarily of projects involving paper. But as my research progressed I realized that the market had exploded with new media for inkjet printers. It's now possible to print on cloth, plastic, transparencies, magnets, fine arts papers and stickers. Computer printed art can be attached to wood, metal, plastic, glass and cloth. The possibilities for arts and crafts appear to be limitless.

In writing this book, I've had three groups of readers in mind: computer users who want to get back to crafting; crafters who want to learn more about computers; and students, teachers and parents who want to know more about both.

• Professional graphic designers have been immersed in the digital world since 1985. As the Internet continues to grow and much design is seen only on-screen, the desire for art you can hold in your hand gets stronger, doesn't it? I hope you'll find lots of excuses to try the projects in this book and liberate the scissors and glue from the back of your drawer. Many of the ideas in this book will work well to create promotional gifts and displays for yourself and your clients.

• Many people enjoy doing handcrafts as a hobby or for a living. More and more of you are coming to realize that a personal computer, along with a scanner and printer, can help take your work to a new level. If you've hesitated about buying a computer, or if you have one but feel awkward using it, I hope this book will help you feel more at ease in the digital world. I am not a computer science major. I am self-taught and have built up my computer skills gradually over the years. Believe me, if you can sew a dress from a pattern or build a birdhouse from plans, you can learn to be a proficient user of computer graphics software. If you need more guidance, take a class or ask your children or grandchildren to help you.

• Eager students, from kindergarten through college, love getting their hands on computers. My own three children taught themselves to use my Macintosh and are fearless in pushing its limits. Kids, here's a whole book full of skills and projects you can use to make fun stuff and change the world. Parents and teachers, why not offer a special elective or workshop in computer arts and crafts? Arts projects teach computer skills in an enjoyable way and help children express their interests and creativity. Here is your text book.

I HOPE THIS BOOK WILL INSPIRE all my readers to be creative—to gather your materials, rally your skills, think about the task at hand and then let the solutions swirl through your brain. What a pleasure it is to feel creative ideas emerge and then be able to execute them. A psychologist coined the term "flow" to express the peak experience that occurs when we are working on a problem that requires just the right amount of mental effort. When problems are too simple, we're bored. When they're too hard, we're overwhelmed. But when the amount of patience, skill, ingenuity, perseverance and work required is just right, then we're "in the flow." I hope *The Arts and Crafts Computer* will be not too little and not too much, but just right for you.

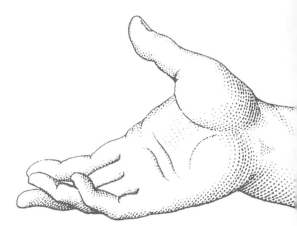

No machine can compare with a person's hands. Machinery gives speed, power, complete uniformity, and precision, but it cannot give creativity, adaptability, freedom, heterogeneity. These the machine is incapable of, hence the superiority of the hand, which no amount of rationalism can negate. People prefer the creative and the free to the fixed and standardized.
—Soetsu Yanagi, *The Unknown Craftsman: A Japanese Insight into Beauty*, 1972

1 Understanding Digital Tools

Every industry, every process, is wrought by a hand, or by a superhand—a machine whose mighty arm and cunning fingers the human hand invents and wields.

—Helen Keller, "The Hand of the World," *American Magazine*, December 1912

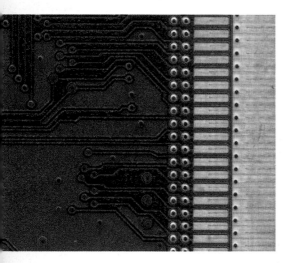

Computing with chips
This detail of a computer circuit board was created by placing the actual board on a scanner. Outmoded circuit boards are sometimes used to create recycled art works.

RE YOU "COMPUTER LITERATE?" Over the past twenty years computers have become pervasive in American life. But for artists and others who value working with their hands, these machines may seem foreign and unnecessary. As a musician friend laments, "It was bad enough when I was a nineteenth century person living in the twentieth century; now I'm a nineteenth century person living in the twenty-first century!" Even so, a personal computer can be a wonderful artist's tool—especially when used along with traditional media. For those of you who have taken the plunge, this chapter will unveil some of the mysteries of computer graphics that may have puzzled you. For those of you who are computer novices, I hope this chapter will nudge you toward becoming computer literate artists.

Choosing a Computer

If you're trying to decide what sort of computer equipment to buy, I highly recommend that you take a beginning computer class at a community college or ask your computer-literate friends to let you try out their systems. One of the first questions to consider is whether you want a Macintosh or a PC.

Macintosh versus PC/Windows

The two main types of personal computer are the Macintosh from Apple and IBM computers or their clones (from companies such as Dell, Compaq and Gateway). An IBM-type computer is also known as a "PC."

HOW MACS EVOLVED

The Macintosh, introduced by Apple in 1984, was radically different from other computers because it had a "graphical interface." Instead of having to type in keyboard commands, Mac users could click and drag *icons* on the computer screen using a small hand-held *mouse* sliding on a pad. Icons represent computer disks, tools and files, including *programs* (or *applications*) and *documents*. The Macintosh became the favorite of professional graphic designers and changed the printing and publishing industries. The first graphics programs—MacPaint, PixelPaint, Photoshop, PageMaker, Illustrator, FreeHand—were developed for the Macintosh. Apple was also first to take advantage of the PostScript graphics language.

HOW WINDOWS EVOLVED

The Mac's easy, visual way of working is called "intuitive" and was so successful that other companies went to work trying to imitate it. The winner was Microsoft Corporation's Windows operating system, which makes it possible for PCs to operate in a way that's similar to Macs. Today the major graphics programs are available in Windows versions and they work pretty much as in their native Mac environment.

A PERSONAL CHOICE

I've used a Macintosh since 1986 and think it's the best computer for graphics. Windows is not as intuitive and easy to learn as the Mac system it imitates, but Macintosh computers are more expensive. So try out both systems and see which one you like best. If you've already chosen, rest assured that you can do all the projects in this book with either a Mac or a PC.

Computer size and speed

Computer equipment keeps getting faster and cheaper—a great trend, but also frustrating since better models always seems to appear right after we buy ours. Get a computer with as much speed and memory as you can afford, and plan to upgrade your system every few years or as your needs change.

PROCESSOR SPEED

A computer's *processor* is a chip (also known as the CPU or *central processing unit*) that does the actual "computing." The faster the processor's *clock rate*, the faster the computer will work. Processor speed is measured in *megahertz* (millions of *Hertz*, MHz), with a Hertz (Hz) being one cycle per second. By comparison, the electrical current that pulses through our homes alternates at 60 Hz, while audible sounds are in the kilohertz range (KHz or thousands of cycles per second). The fastest personal computers run at over 1000 MHz (1000 million cycles per second), making them very fast calculators indeed!

COMPUTER MEMORY

Memory is a computer's capacity to store information on a *chip*. It's measured in *bits* and *bytes* going up in multiples of 1024 to *kilobytes, megabytes* and *gigabytes*. Memory is different from *storage* (see below). The two kinds of memory in computers are RAM and ROM.

Random-access memory (RAM) is used for calculations in "real time" (right now). When you shut the computer off, whatever information was stored in RAM disappears. It's similar to short-term memory in a human being. The more RAM you have, the better you'll be able to work on graphic images, which tend to be large and "memory-intensive." A typical personal computer is equipped with 64 MB of RAM. Additional RAM chips can purchased and installed, usually in 128 MB increments. Computers also include *read-only memory* or ROM which is used for storing information that is rarely changed, such as the operating system.

Storage capacity

Long-term storage of computer information is done either magnetically on *disks* or tapes or optically on *optical disks* or *CD-ROM disks*. Computers include an internal storage disk—sometimes called the *hard disk*—which can range in size from 500 MB to 60 GB. Computers also use external storage drives and media including floppy disks (from 800K to 1200 K), zip disks (100 MB to 250 MB), CD-ROM disks (up to 700 MB), optical disks (from about 600 MB to 9 GB) and external (auxiliary) hard disks (6 GB to 68 GB). The more storage capacity you have, the more *applications* you will be able to install and use and the more documents (such as graphic images) you will be able to save.

From Looms to Computers

Craftspeople have used machines as aids for thousands of years. The woodcut below, made by German artist Jost Amman in 1568, illustrates a weaving loom of the time. For hundreds of years the weaving of cloth for clothing and household use was done at home by artisans using wooden, hand-powered looms. But weaving was one of the first home industries to be mechanized during the Industrial Revolution, causing unemployment, social upheaval and disruption of family life as jobs moved from the home to factories. British handicraftsmen opposed to factory weaving formed groups known as Luddites, which rioted against the factories and were brutally repressed by around 1816. *Luddite* is still used as a term to describe a person who is opposed to the use of machines or technology, such as computers. Ironically, the first computers grew directly from the weaving industry. A Frenchman named Jacquard used punched cards to mechanize the creation of patterns in factory woven cloth. Jacquard's work influenced Englishman Charles Babbage, who developed the first calculating machine around 1841. He was aided by Ada Lovelace, a brilliant mathematician and daughter of the poet Lord Byron. A software language developed by the U.S. Department of Defense was named Ada in her honor in 1979.

A

B

C

D

Bitmaps and PostScript

A bitmap, such as this scan of an initial capital, is made up of many small pixels. At a resolution of 266 ppi, the pixels are not visible when the scan is printed at actual size (**A**), but when it's enlarged to 250 percent the image loses quality (**B**). By contrast, a PostScript version (made by autotracing the scan) has the same smoothness at small (**C**) and large sizes (**D**).

Understanding Bitmaps and PostScript

The two main graphics formats on personal computers are bitmaps and vectors.

Bitmapped graphics

A *bitmap* is an image made up of a grid of *bits* or *dots*, much as an Impressionist painting is made up of small brush strokes. At close range a bitmap looks like rows of differently colored square tiles, but from further back the grid "disappears" and we see an image. All scanned images, digital camera images, and images created in a "paint" or image-editing program such as Photoshop are bitmaps.

ADVANTAGES AND DISADVANTAGES OF BITMAPS

• Bitmaps are good at reproducing images that contain lots of detail and soft, painterly effects, such as photographs and scanned artwork.

• Editing changes made to a bitmap (such as applying a texture, for example) will apply to the entire image (or whatever portions of it have been "selected"). But the computer does not distinguish different pictorial elements of an image. For example, the computer doesn't know that a bitmap contains a green tree against a blue sky. It only knows that certain pixels in the bitmap are green and certain others are blue. So to edit the tree alone, without effecting the sky, we have to "select" the tree by drawing around it, which can be a laborious process.

• Bitmaps cannot be enlarged without losing quality, since enlarging does not increase the number of pixels but only makes the pixels larger, in effect. So if a scan or digital camera image does not produce a good quality print, it will have to be scanned again at a higher resolution or size.

Vector and PostScript graphics

Vector graphics make it possible to represent graphic elements as "objects." Each element of a vector graphic—a circle, a square, a line and so on—is represented by a mathematical description rather than by a grid of pixels. *PostScript* is a powerful programming language that dominates the vector graphics software field. PostScript graphics can be printed smoothly at any resolution without visible stair-stepping of edges. This happens because each time a PostScript document is printed it is "redrawn" to take advantage of the resolution of the printer. PostScript is best for printing text and for creating technical drawings. It can also be used to create illustrations, but not with the soft textural effects found in "painted" bitmaps.

ADVANTAGES AND DISADVANTAGES OF POSTSCRIPT

• The elements of a PostScript illustration are separate and can be selected easily and edited independently. But it's harder to apply overall effects to a PostScript illustration that's composed of many separate elements.

• A PostScript illustration can be printed at the same quality at any size, at whatever resolutions are provided by the printer. The same small and compact PostScript document used to print a logo on a business card can also print it at billboard size.

• PostScript illustrations tend to be hard-edged and mechanical-looking.

Glossary of Common Computer Terms

application
A software program used to create and modify documents, for example for word processing, graphics, page layout and so on.

ASCII
Short for "American standard code for information interchange," a system that uses code numbers to refer to letters, numbers and common symbols. Text files saved in ASCII format can be transferred between Macs and PCs.

binary
A number system based on two digits (0 and 1), as opposed to the decimal system (10 digits) used in arithmetic. Computers use the binary system for calculating.

bit
Short for "binary digit"; the smallest unit of computer information. Based on a binary number system, a bit can be either 0 or 1.

bitmap
A grid of bits or pixels making up a graphic image.

byte
A unit of computer information containing eight bits; capable of encoding 256 different "characters," such as numbers and letters. Also, **kilobyte** (1024 bytes, abbreviated KB), **megabyte** (1024KB or 1,048,576 bytes; abbreviated MB in writing and "meg" in speech) and **gigabyte** (1024 MB or 1,073,741,824 bytes, abbreviated GB in writing and "gig" in speech). The prefixes *kilo*, *mega* and *giga* mean *thousand*, *great* and *giant*, respectively.

CCD
Short for "charge-coupled device," an array of tiny elements, mounted on a chip, that measure the intensity of light and convert that to digital information. Used in scanners and digital cameras to convert light information into digital data.

chip
A tiny piece of silicon containing a pattern of impurities that creates a miniature electrical circuit.

clock rate
The fundamental rate, measured in cycles per second, at which a computer processor performs its most basic operations, such as adding two numbers.

disk
A coated, round platter on which computer information is stored magnetically or optically.

document
A computer file created by an application and saved under a single name; for example, a scanned photo or a letter typed in a word processing program.

dot
A small circle or ellipse that is the smallest unit of a printed graphic.

dpi
Dots per inch, a measure of printer resolution.

EPS
Short for "encapsulated PostScript"; a format for saving PostScript documents.

file
A collection of information that has one name; can be either a document (such as a scan of a photo) or an application (such as an image-editing program).

hard disk or hard drive
A non-removable disk inside a computer, used for long-term storage of data.

Hertz
One cycle, occurrence, alteration or pulse per second; named after the German physicist, Heinrich Rudolph Hertz (1857–1894).

icon
An on-screen symbol that represents a file, a folder, a disk or a tool.

memory
Computer information electronically stored on a chip.

mouse
A small hand-held device with a roller ball and a clicker which, when moved around on a flat horizontal surface, correspondingly moves the icons and pointers on a computer monitor screen. Optical mice are also becoming common.

native format
The format in which an application usually saves documents, as opposed to a standard format such as PICT or TIFF.

operating system
The basic software that makes a computer operate.

PICT
A standard Macintosh file format for low-resolution (72 dpi or less) bitmapped graphics; short for "picture."

pixel
Short for "picture element"; a small square that is the smallest element of a bitmapped image.

PostScript
A "page-description language" used to represent the lines, curves and solid areas that make up the text and graphics on a computer "page."

program
Instructions that tell a computer what to do; same as software, but used differently in speech and writing. For example, "The amount of software needed to create computer graphics consists of about four main programs."

RAM
Short for "random access memory"; computer memory used for short-term tasks, not for long-term storage.

resolution
The number of pixels per square inch in a digital image, expressed as ppi; the higher the ppi, the better the resolution of the image.

RGB
Short for "red, green and blue"; a color model used for computer monitors (and television screens) in which all the colors of the rainbow are created by mixing red, green and blue light.

ROM
Short for "read-only memory"; computer memory used for storage of system software and other elements that are not changed often; information can be read *from* it, but new information cannot be read *to* it (i.e. recorded onto it).

software
Instructions that tell a computer what to do. Often used to designate computer programs in general as in, "The price of software is going up."

TIFF
Short for "tagged image file format"; a standard format for saving high-resolution (higher than 72 dpi) bitmapped images.

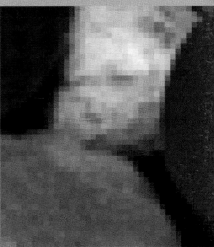

Grids of pixels
Digital images (such as this scanned photo of vegetables from the farmers' market) are made up of a grid of tiny square pixels. Up close they look like rows of differently colored square tiles, but from a distance the pixels appear to blend into a coherent image.

Choosing Software for Graphics

The two main types of graphics applications—those used for painting and image-editing (using bitmaps) and those used for vector or PostScript drawing—used to be quite distinct. But as software has developed over the past fifteen years, painting programs have come to include some "drawing" functions (such as scaling and rotating, for example), and drawing programs have come to include some "painting" functions (such as layering and the use of textural filters). But the main difference between the two remains that painting programs use bitmaps and most drawing programs use PostScript.

Painting and image-editing

Painting and image-editing programs are used to create original bitmapped images and also to edit images that have been captured with a scanner or a digital camera. A painting program typically contains a toolbox full of functions that imitate conventional artist's tools, such as pencils, brushes and paint. Image-editing programs also contain tools for adjusting contrast, focus and color and many include "filters" for applying special effects. Most of the projects in this book involve using an image-editing program.

Photoshop is acknowledged as the premier image-editing program for personal computers. It was developed by Adobe Systems primarily for editing scanned photos and many of its functions are based on traditional darkroom techniques. Photoshop is a complex and sophisticated program with many powerful functions and is a mainstay for people who work in newspaper and magazine publishing and for the Internet. However, one need not know Photoshop inside-out to be able to use it effectively. Straightforward operations—such as correcting contrast, sharpening focus or removing a color cast—are handled in an intuitive way and can be easily mastered. If you want a program that can do basic image-editing *and* go beyond this to alter and enhance your images with maximum flexibility and range,

I recommend using Photoshop. I've used it for this book and for all the image-editing in my six previous books on computer graphics. However, Photoshop is expensive—version 6 sold for $600 as this book was being written. Adobe has recently released a less expensive version called Photoshop Elements which sells for around $100. It compares well with the other less expensive and less complex image-editing programs available for both Macs and PCs. These programs provide enough tools for basic editing and improvement of photographs and can be used to create most of the projects in this book. They include CorelPHOTOPAINT, Paint Shop Pro and Deneba Canvas (which also includes vector drawing functions).

Painterly effects with bitmaps

Bitmapped programs used for computer "painting" are surprisingly good at imitating the effects of traditional artist materials such as pastels and paint. I used a real pencil to make a black-and-white drawing for a children's book illustration, then scanned the drawing and opened it in Painter to add color. I started with soft color areas made with a dry brush (top), applied darker shaded areas with a chalk tool (center) and added final details with lighter strokes. Some final filter effects were applied in Photoshop (bottom).

Painter is a "natural media" painting program with hundreds of specialized brushes that imitate traditional artist materials including oil, acrylic, watercolor, pastel, colored pencil and so on. It also includes special cloning tools that imitate the brush work of Van Gogh and Seurat. Images created in Painter and printed on high-quality watercolor paper or canvas can barely be distinguished from traditional art work.

PostScript illustration

PostScript illustration programs were developed primarily for technical illustration, but they can also be used to create patterns and illustrations that are richly colorful and imaginative. The tools and commands make it possible to create geometrical shapes (ovals, rectangles, stars, spirals), draw "paths" (including lines and curves), "transform" shapes and paths by scaling, rotating, skewing and reflecting (flipping across an axis), apply solid fills and outlines to shapes and to create smooth blends (gradients) between colors. It's also possible to import a scanned photo to use as a drawing guide. PostScript illustration programs can also be used to create and manipulate PostScript type and are especially good for the creation of business logos. Adobe Illustrator was the first PostScript illustration program to be developed, followed quickly by Macromedia FreeHand and CorelDRAW. Illustrator is the biggest seller of the three and works especially well with Photoshop, since both are made by Adobe Systems.

Self-expression must pass into communication for its fulfillment…
—Pearl S. Buck,
In Search of Readers, 1950

Smooth shapes with PostScript
PostScript illustration programs excel at creating and manipulating geometrical shapes. I took advantage of that when creating this mandala, which includes many repeated elements (top). PostScript programs also make it possible to create *gradients* (blends from one color to another) that produce a glowing effect that's similar to airbrushing. I filled my mandala shapes with both solid colors and gradients (bottom left), then quickly created a new look by editing the gradients to produce different color blends (bottom right). The mandalas were created in Illustrator.

Virtual Visual Worlds

The appearance of the display on a computer monitor is based on an interaction between technology and the human visual system. If the monitor has enough displayed points (pixels) and the screen pattern is refreshed at least 25 times per second, then we humans can integrate this dot pattern into a stable, continuous image. Quivering horizontal bands of light would appear across the screen if the refresh rate were slower. So the image we see on a computer or TV screen is an illusion or technical magic trick.

In the same way, our view of the real world is a magic trick based on the way light reflected from objects interacts with the rows of rods and cones in our eyes and the way our brains interpret and present this data.

All worlds are virtual worlds, in a sense, and the Eastern philosophical view of reality as *maya* or a veil of illusion is scientifically true, at least so far as perception is concerned. But these illusions look convincingly real and our perceptions provide us with pleasure and pain, despite their mysterious underpinnings.

Page layout programs

A page layout program is used to create publications—from a flyer to a multi-page magazine or book—by making it possible to combine type and graphics and to manipulate the size and position of these elements. Page layout programs are based on PostScript and use smooth-printing PostScript fonts. But bitmaps created in an image-editing program—such as scanned photos—can be imported for use as illustrations.

PageMaker was the first PostScript page layout program, followed by QuarkXPress, which now is the biggest seller. Adobe acquired PageMaker and also produces a new program, InDesign, designed to compete with Quark.

Some word-processing programs, such as Word and Word Perfect, can also import graphics and create Post-Script type and can be used to design pages, but not with as much freedom and ease as in a page layout program.

Hand-drawing with a computer

Once you have a computer and a graphics program, how do you actually draw or paint? There are two ways to draw on a computer—with a mouse or with a stylus.

USING THE MOUSE

"Drawing with a mouse is like drawing with a bar of soap," says John Odam, my co-author on *Start with a Scan* (Peachpit Press, 2000). The mouse was developed primarily for interaction with icons and while it's possible to draw with it—I do it every day—it's clumsy. If you plan to do a lot of drawing and painting on-screen, you may want to invest in a tablet and stylus.

USING A DIGITIZING TABLET AND STYLUS

A pressure-sensitive plastic tablet, shaped like a rectangular mouse pad, is connected to the computer. You hold a stylus shaped like a pen, and as you draw with it on the tablet, your on-screen tool moves accordingly. The stylus makes it possible to draw more smoothly and to take advantage of your conventional drawing skills. In addition, the tablet is sensitive to the amount of pressure you put on the stylus. The harder you press, the thicker and darker

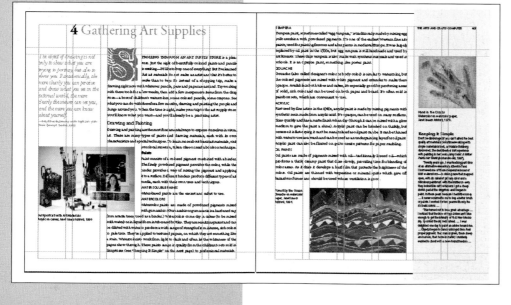

Combining text and graphics
Page layout programs make it possible to combine text, headlines and graphics to create designed pages. *The Arts and Crafts Computer* was created in PageMaker. A screen shot of the layout for the opening pages of Chapter 4 shows the six-column grid structure that I used to organize the pages. Grids and guidelines can be easily specified to help in the positioning of text and graphic elements. For more information on grids see page 58.

your on-screen mark will be (provided you are using an application that's designed to take advantage of this feature). The natural-media brushes in Painter, for example, work especially well with a pressure-sensitive tablet and stylus, making it almost like drawing and painting with traditional media.

Understanding Resolution

Resolution is a measure of any system's ability to display fine detail, whether it be in a computer or in the human eye. In computer graphics, resolution refers to the number of small units—dots or pixels—making up an image. The more units per inch, the finer the image will be and the more accurate it will look.

Types of resolution

Resolution means different things when applied to monitors, digital images and printers. Taking time now to understand each kind of resolution will help prevent confusion later on and help you get the best results with scanning and printing.

MONITOR RESOLUTION

Attached to a computer is a TV-like monitor on which images are displayed. The resolution of a monitor is determined by how many pixels per inch (ppi) are displayed on the screen. Monitor resolution on a PC is generally 96 ppi and on a Mac is generally 72 ppi. (Apple chose 72 ppi because type is traditionally measured in "points," with 72 points to an inch.) These resolutions are fairly low, compared with the 150 ppi to 300 ppi usually used for scanned images, but the quality of an on-screen image depends not only on the number

of pixels per inch but on the "bit depth" of each pixel; that is, how many bits of information are assigned to each one. An 8-bit monitor can assign one of 256 different colors or shades of gray to each pixel, but a 24-bit monitor can choose from among 16.7 million. So a scanned photo will look better on a 24-bit than on an 8-bit monitor because its colors are more truly represented, even though the number of pixels is the same.

IMAGE RESOLUTION

Image resolution (expressed in ppi) measures the number of pixels per inch. The more pixels, the higher the resolution and the more detailed the image will be. Image resolution is usually higher than monitor resolution, but

Monitor versus print resolution
When an image will be viewed only on-screen, as with the Internet, it need not have an image resolution any higher than the monitor resolution. But when graphics are to be printed, then image resolution should be higher. This scan of a painting—"Cape Plein Air" by the late Mendocino, California artist Olaf Palm—was taken from a Web page. It is 6.5 inches wide, has a resolution of 72 ppi and looks all right when printed at about a third of its actual size (above). But when printed a 100 percent of its actual size, the low resolution produces a lower quality image (left). This image Is reproduced courtesy of Jennifer Palm.

Watch out for the jaggies!
Frank Lloyd Wright built a second home called Taliesen West near Phoenix, Arizona. This photo of it was scanned at 266 ppi and is printed on this page at actual size (above, right). At this size and resolution the scan has good quality. However, look what happens when the very same scan is enlarged on the page to 700 percent its actual size. The pixels making up the image become visible, resulting in "jaggies" or stair-stepping, especially on diagonal edges.

no matter how high the resolution of an image, it will still be displayed on your monitor at either 72 ppi (on a MAC) or 96 ppi (on a PC). You will not see full detail until it's printed by a high-resolution printer.

PRINTER RESOLUTION

Printer resolution—expressed as *dpi* or dots per inch—measures the number of dots of ink the printer lays down on the paper. As you may already know, graphic images are printed by converting their colors or gray tones into a grid of dots. You can see these dots by looking at a printed photo (in a magazine, for example) with a printer's *loupe* or a magnifying glass. Printer resolution is often higher than image resolution because it can take several printer "dots" to represent one image "pixel."

Areas of confusion

Resolution can be confusing. The terms dpi and ppi are often used interchangeably, even though they have different meanings. *Pixels are the smallest units in a digital image, whereas dots are the smallest units in a printed image.* Also, a dot is not always the same size as a pixel. So when a 240 ppi image, for example, is printed at 720 dpi on a color inkjet printer, the printer creates very small dots (at a rate of 720 per inch) to accurately represent all the color information in each pixel (which in a 24-bit image could be any one of over 16.7 million colors).

WHAT IS LINESCREEN?

Another variable that effects resolution is "linescreen" or lines per inch (lpi). Linescreen (also called "frequency") is a printing-industry term that refers to the number of lines of dots (both vertical and horizontal) per inch in a halftone screen. A halftone screen is a pattern of dots used to represent the smooth tones of an image. The screen is used to make a printing plate, which prints the small dots on paper where they blend to create a smooth-looking image.

In commercial printing, linescreens range from the coarse 85 lpi used for newspapers (which can be seen without magnification) to the fine 200 lpi used for high-quality color art books. (A linescreen of 133 lpi is considered to be the resolution of the normal human eye.) As computers have come to be used for making halftone screens, a rule of thumb has evolved: Image resolution (in ppi) should equal two times the linescreen (lpi) of the printer. (For example, this book was printed with a linescreen of 133 lpi, so I used an image resolution of 266 ppi for most of the artwork.) But the projects described in this book are made using personal printers rather than printing presses. So do we still need to be concerned with linescreen? Yes, because personal printers also create halftone screens at particular linescreen frequencies. For laser printers we should follow the rule and make the image resolution be twice the linescreen. But there's a different formula for inkjet printers, because of the way their dots tend to spread on paper. Follow the guidelines in the sidebar on the right. For more information and guidelines for commercial printing see *The Non-Designer's Scan and Print Book* by Sandee Cohen and Robin Williams (Peachpit Press, 2000).

Guidelines for Resolution

Image resolution always involves a trade-off between quality and document size, since the higher the resolution the larger the document will be and the more computer resources it will use. It doesn't make sense to create images at resolutions higher than your printer can use.

For bitmapped images that are to be printed by offset lithography (a photo in a magazine, for example) a resolution of 250 ppi to 300 ppi at actual size is usually enough to produce a good quality image. But the projects in this book will be printed primarily on desktop printers—inkjet and laser printers—which have lower resolution requirements, so resolutions of 100 ppi to 150 ppi will usually be high enough, so long as the image is printed at its actual size.

Below are formulae for getting the best printed results with the lowest resolution. These formulae assume that images are printed at "actual size."

Printing black-and-white (1-bit) bitmaps on laser printers
image resolution = printer resolution
For 1-bit raster images (in which all the pixels are either 100 percent black or 100 percent white) use exactly the same resolution for the image as for the printer. For example, to print on a laser printer at 600 dpi, scan black-and-white line art at 600 ppi.

Printing grayscale or color bitmaps on laser printers
image resolution = 2 x lpi
The linescreen of most laser printers is either 65 lpi or 85 lpi, so optimum image resolution for laser output would be 130 ppi or 170 ppi, regardless of whether you're printing at 300 dpi or 1200 dpi. Linescreen is sometimes listed in the printer's specifications. If it's not, assume the higher linescreen and create images at 170 ppi.

Printing grayscale or color bitmaps on inkjet printers
image resolution = ¹/₃ printer resolution
The rules are different for inkjet printers because the ink dots tend to spread. Epson recommends that image resolution be no more than ¹/₃ the printer resolution. So to print at 720 dpi, for example, the image resolution should be 240 ppi.

Printing PostScript art
PostScript images are optimized to print at any resolution provided by the printer. So if you specify 600 dpi, for example, the PostScript language code embedded in your document will draw the image to fit that resolution and take full advantage of its fineness.

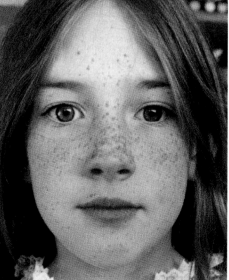

From photos to halftone screens
To print a photograph on a printing press, the image must first be broken up into small "halftone" dots. The number of lines of dots per inch in a halftone is referred to as "linescreen" or lpi (lines per inch). At a linescreen of 133, my daughter Florrie's face looks smooth (right), but is actually made up of thousands of small dots printed in four colors of ink (cyan, magenta, yellow and black), which overlap to produce all the colors in the original (above). Look at any printed image with a magnifying glass and you will clearly see the halftone dots that make up the image.

Computer Comfort and Safety

Computers are wonderful, powerful tools, but their use can be physically hazardous to human beings in at least three ways: 1) Working at a computer for long periods of time can cause eyestrain and injury to muscles in the back, neck, shoulders, arms and hands; 2) Computers emit harmful electromagnetic radiation (as do all machines that use electricity); 3) The manufacturing of computers involves materials which harm workers and the environment, both during the manufacturing process and later when computers are disposed of in landfills.

Computer ergonomics

Ergonomics is the study of how human bodies are affected by our work and our use of various tools. Poor posture and habits at home, play or work can cause injuries such as "tennis elbow" or "carpal tunnel syndrome." Working at a computer for long periods of time can cause various problems including eyestrain and muscle aches and injury. Taking the time to create an *ergonomically sound workstation* will help prevent headaches and muscle pain. Three important aspects of safe, comfortable computer use are good equipment, good positioning and good work habits.

Use the right equipment

It's worth it to invest in good quality equipment that can be adjusted to fit the guidelines shown in the diagram.

Get a good computer chair

A good-quality adjustable office chair is essential for computer use. Find one with these features:
• adjustable chair back with support for your lower back
• well-padded seat with soft, curved front edge
• adjustable height
• five legs with rollers for easy and safe maneuverability
• room (1 to 4 inches) between the front edge of the seat and the back of your knees
• no chair arms or else arms that don't interfere with comfortable typing and mousing

Use a good work surface

A strong, stable computer work surface should have these features:
• large enough surface area for your monitor and all other equipment to be within easy reach; the computer itself can go on the floor if necessary
• height of 28 inches to 32 inches from the floor, so that surface is approximately at elbow level

Use equipment correctly

Avoid strain to eyes and muscles by positioning your table surface, chair, keyboard and mouse, monitor and other materials (papers you are viewing, telephone and so on) so that all are within easy sight and reach.

Relax your arms and shoulders

Make sure that when you are typing or mousing, your shoulders are relaxed (not scrunched up), your arms are at your sides, and your elbows are bent at a 90 degree angle. If your table is too high to allow this, raise your chair.

Protect your hands and wrists

Position your computer keyboard and mouse so that when you type or use the mouse your hands are in a "neutral" position (forearm, wrist and hand in a straight line, parallel with the floor). If your keyboard is too high, raise your chair. Another option is to lower your desk or use a desk with a lowered keyboard tray. Make sure the tray has room for both the keyboard and your mouse and mouse pad. Position the keyboard and mouse so that they're directly in front, close to you and at the same height.

Support your legs and back

Make sure your table surface provides comfortable space above the tops of your thighs, your thighs are parallel with the floor and your feet are flat on the floor. If your feet are off the floor because you've raised your chair height to get a good typing position, then use an adjustable foot rest.

Prevent eyestrain

The top your monitor screen should be level with your eyes, so that you work with your head up straight, eyes looking slightly downward toward the center of the screen. Position the monitor at arm's length away from your body (both for viewing ease and radiation safety). Keep your screen clean by wiping it regularly with glass cleaner. If necessary, eliminate glare from windows or room lights by using an antiglare shield. Adjust the contrast and brightness of the monitor so that it's easy to view and read. If you wear bifocals and find yourself moving your head up and down to read the screen, consider having special glasses made for computer use.

Learn to touch type, to avoid looking back and forth between keyboard and monitor too much. If you refer to papers a lot, lean them upright against a copy stand or put them in a document holder next to the monitor, at about the same distance and height as the monitor. Rest your eyes periodically by focusing on an object at least 20 feet away. Blink often.

Develop good work habits

Different people are affected differently by computer use depending on their age, physical fitness, health conditions (for example pregnancy or diabetes), other hobbies and activities (such as playing a musical instrument), and also their ability to relax and get along with others. The following guidelines will help you be aware of work habits and attitudes that promote comfort, relaxation, health and safety.

Vary your work day

Sitting still for long periods or performing repetitive tasks is unnatural for human beings. Our bodies work best when we move often and perform a variety of different activities.
• Take a break from the computer every 20 or 30 minutes ideally, but at the very least every hour.
• Take frequent breaks to get up and walk around, bend and stretch and rest

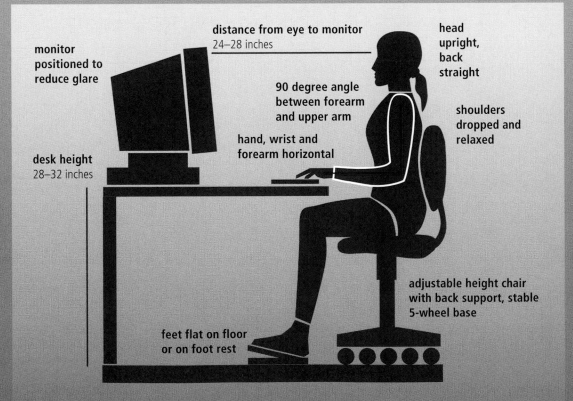

monitor positioned to reduce glare

desk height 28–32 inches

distance from eye to monitor 24–28 inches

90 degree angle between forearm and upper arm

hand, wrist and forearm horizontal

head upright, back straight

shoulders dropped and relaxed

adjustable height chair with back support, stable 5-wheel base

feet flat on floor or on foot rest

your eyes. Frequent short breaks may be of greater value than fewer, longer breaks.
• Use a timer or reminder software to remind you to take breaks.
• Do a variety of tasks during the day.
• Don't push yourself to keep working if you're having pain or discomfort.

Relieve your stress
• Remember to relax your shoulders and hands while working.
• Several times a day take a break to practice calming, deep breathing exercises.
• Avoid working overtime.
• Be especially careful to pace yourself when working under deadline pressure.
• Be aware of the effects of stress. From time to time take inventory of the stress in your life and change what you are able to change.
• Be aware of the physical effects of all your other activities (sports, hobbies, and so on) to avoid repetitive stressful movements.
• Strengthen your body and relieve stress by making exercise an everyday part of your life. Include aerobic exercise (such as brisk walking), bending and stretching (such as yoga or tai chi) and weight training (such as push-ups).

Resources on ergonomics

Web sites
• Ergonomics Program
UC San Francisco, UC Berkeley
www.me.berkeley.edu/ergo/
• ErgoWorld
www.home.earthlink.net/~ergo1/
An office ergonomics section includes links to resources on reducing eye strain, avoiding carpal tunnel syndrome, typing injury, posture and so on.
• Yale University Ergonomics
www.yale.edu/ergo
Includes a printable Ergonomics Catalog with listings and suppliers for equipment such as foot rests, glare screens, copy stands and so on.

Books
• *Healing Back Pain: The Mind-Body Connection,* John E. Sarno, M.D. Warner Books, 1991
Presents the idea that most chronic back, neck and shoulder pain is not caused by physical injury but by repressed emotions and proposes a psychological treatment without drugs, surgery or exercise.
• *The Hand Book: Preventing Computer Injury*
Stephanie Brown
Ergonomie, New York, 1992

Hazards of electromagnetic radiation
In response to concerns about radiation emissions from computers, especially from the TV-like monitor (also called a VDT, or "video display terminal") some manufacturers have reduced emission levels to conform to the "Swedish Standards." These include the MPR II standards, which set limits on electric and magnetic field emissions in the ELF (extremely low frequency) and VLF (very low frequency) ranges, as well as the electrostatic field. More recent standards, promoted by the Swedish Confederation of Professional Employees (TCO), expanded in 1995, also include guidelines for energy consumption, screen flicker, luminance and keyboard use. Before buying new computer equipment, you may want to find out whether it conforms to the MPR II and TCO 95 standards.
• It's recommended that you sit at least two feet away from the front of your monitor and at least four feet away from the sides and back of a monitor. Classrooms with rows of computers should be set up to provide that much space for all users.

Resource
TCO (Swedish Confederation of Professional Employees)
TCO Development, U.S. office
150 N. Michigan Ave., Suite 1200
Chicago, IL 60601
312/781-6223
www.tcodevelopment.com
TCO Development works on quality certification and environmental labeling of office equipment including computers, monitors and keyboards.

Hazards of manufacturing computers
Hundreds of hazardous chemicals and other materials are used in the manufacturing of computers and other digital devices. These materials are harmful to the health of the workers who use them and often end up in local water supplies, harming people in nearby communities. In addition, when computers are disposed of in landfills, their hazardous materials can leach into the environment. Computer monitors contain lead and brominated flame retardants, batteries contain mercury, circuit boards have cadmium and cables and casings use PVC plastics. The National Safety Council estimates that around 300 million personal computers will become obsolete over the next four years and most will be dumped in the trash. Consumer groups are calling for the reduction in use of hazardous materials in computers, the ability to more easily upgrade computers and the ability to return old computers back to their producers for safe reuse and recycling.

It's estimated that of the over 24 million computers thrown away in the U.S. in 1999, only 14 percent were disposed of properly or recycled. In Spring 2000, Massachusetts became the first state to make recycling of monitors and TVs mandatory. Goodwill stores and Salvation Army sites signed up to receive old equipment and either sell it or recycle it according to state standards. Nationwide, Goodwill Industries receives more than 100,000 computers a year, though they may not accept the oldest, outmoded models.

Resources on recycling
Computers for Schools Association
www.detwiler.org

Computers for Youth
www.cfy.org

Goodwill Industries Int'l, Inc.
9200 Rockville Pike
Bethesda, MD 20814
301/530-6500
www.goodwill.org
Goodwill repairs and resells donated computers and also participates in recycling programs.

IBM PC Recycling Service
www.ibm.com/environment
888/746-7426
In November 2000, IBM announced a PC recycling service through which individual consumers can send back any manufacturer's computer equipment for a fee of $29.99, which includes shipping. IBM will either recycle the equipment or refurbish and arrange for its donation to Gifts in Kind International (GIKI). If the computer meets the criteria for donation, the donor will receive a receipt for potential deduction on their annual federal tax return up to the amount allowed by law.

Massachusetts Department of Environmental Protection
www.state.ma.us/dep/
Provides information on the state's computer recycling program.

Silicon Valley Toxics Coalition
760 N. First Street
San Jose, CA 95112
408/287-6707
www.svtc.org
Founded in 1982 after the discovery of local groundwater pollution from chemicals used to make semiconductor chips. Works to inform the public about the hazards of computer manufacturing and disposal.

National Cristina Foundation
203/863-9100
www.cristina.org
The NCF receives donations of used computers from businesses and individuals, in order to provide training for people with disabilities, students at risk and economically disadvantaged people.

National Recycling Coalition
703/683-9025
www.nrc-recycle.org

Share the Technology
856/234-6156
www.sharetechnology.org

Bringing Images Into the Computer

Just as real acoustical instruments sound richer and more natural than electronically synthesized sounds, so the art created outside of a computer—either by photography or by drawing and painting—is often richer and more interesting than art created electronically. Bringing these "outside" images into the computer is key to computer graphics sophistication and is done by scanning or using a digital camera.

Using a desktop scanner

A scanner can take a digital "picture" of anything that's placed on its flat glass surface. Flatbed scanners range in price from $100 to $2,000 and some provide adapters for scanning slides. Most come with software for specifying resolution and size and usually include a "plug-in" for scanning directly into an image-editing program, such as Photoshop. Reliable scanners are manufactured by many well-known companies, including Hewlett-Packard, UMAX, Epson, Microtek and Agfa. Check computer magazines such as *Macworld* and *PCWorld* for quality ratings and check the Internet for the lowest prices.

HOW SCANNERS WORK

When you click "scan" in your scanning software, the scanner positions its scanning unit and then moves it slowly across the image-area, under the glass, while lamps containing red, green and blue light shine on whatever original you have placed face down on the glass. The light is reflected onto mirrors which direct it through a lens to a CCD (charge-coupled device) sensor. The sensor translates the light into digital impulses that create a bitmapped image in which the colors in the original are defined by amounts of red, green and blue light, creating what's called an *RGB* image (see "Understanding Color Models" on pages 22–23).

BASICS OF SCANNING

Scanning modes. Most desktop scanners provide at least three scanning modes. Black-and-white mode is used for scanning simple black-and-white line art or text. Grayscale mode is used for black-and-white photos (which contain shades of gray) and also for black-and-white drawings that have fine detail and shading. Color mode is used for color photos and art work.

Bit depth. Each mode has its own "bit depth," which refers to the amount of information stored in each pixel in the image. For example, the bit depth of black-and-white mode is 1 bit, which means that each pixel in a black-and-white image can be either black or white. Grayscale mode produces an 8-bit image, so each pixel can be any one of 256 shades of gray, ranging from white to black. Color scanning with a bit depth of 24 bits will produce a range of 16.7 million possible colors per pixel, making it possible to reproduce photographs with great accuracy.

Scanning resolution. Some desktop scanners can capture images at resolutions up to 600 ppi and above, but resolutions this high are usually not needed when printing is done on an inkjet or laser printer. To determine the best resolution for your purpose, see "Guidelines for Resolution" on page 17.

Photos to go
Many companies provide CD-ROM disks filled with pre-scanned photographs and other art work, much of which is copyright free and can be used in newsletters and flyers as well as for arts and crafts projects such as greeting cards or wrapping paper. The images shown here are from Dynamic Graphics, Inc.

Working with photographs

Photographs are a staple ingredient of computer graphics and can be brought into the computer environment in several different ways.

SCANNING CONVENTIONAL PHOTOS

Prints or slides taken with a conventional camera can be scanned using a desktop scanner. Prints on glossy paper work best. Your roll of film can also be developed, scanned and saved on a CD-ROM disk. Ask about this service at your local film developing outlet. For "almost instant" computer images, you can use a Polaroid camera and scan the prints as soon as they dry. (For more information see "Scanning Traditional Art and Photos" on page 26 and "Basics of Image Editing" on page 31).

USING A DIGITAL CAMERA

For truly instant computer images you can use a digital camera. This new kind of camera uses optics similar to those of conventional cameras, but instead of using film to record the light passing through the lens, a digital camera uses a CCD array (similar to that used in a scanner) to digitize the light information. This data is saved either on the camera's internal memory or on a removable card or disk. The number of pictures that can be taken in a given photo session depends upon the memory storage available. Floppy disks containing photo images can be inserted directly into a computer's disk drive. Images stored in camera memory and on some cards are transferred to the computer via a cable. Other cards use special adaptors or slots.

Digital cameras range in price from about $300 to $1000 and, as with all computer equipment, keep getting better and cheaper. Manufacturers include many of the well-known makers of conventional cameras including Kodak, Sony, Minolta, Olympus, Nikon and Canon. As with scanners, check computer magazines for ratings and check mail-order catalogs and the Internet for the lowest prices.

CD-ROM PHOTO COLLECTIONS

Many companies sell collections of copyright-free photos and other art work, stored on CD-ROM disks. Content ranges from contemporary photography to historical images and fine art. These images are usually saved in several standard formats and can be edited in an image-editing program. See the Resources section for the names of some of the larger stock photo suppliers.

Is it digital or conventional?
The photo at the top was taken with a Minolta 35mm single lens reflex camera, printed on 4-inch by 6-inch glossy photo paper, and scanned at 266 ppi on a Microtek ScanMaker X6EL. The photo below it was taken with a Nikon Coolpix 990 digital camera at its highest image quality and converted to 266 ppi. Both photos were printed on this page at actual size using a linescreen of 133 lpi. In general, I've found that my digital photos tend to be a little paler than those taken with my conventional camera and I usually use Photoshop to increase their saturation (see page 31). Both photos below were edited to adjust their contrast, but no other editing was done.

Understanding Color Models: RGB and CMYK

Sometimes the blue sky in a photo looks bright and clear on the screen but muddy and dull when printed on paper on your inkjet printer. That's because two different **color models**—RGB and CYMK— are used for screen display and for printing. Understanding color models can help you get the best printed colors. (For more information see "Working with Color" on page 54.)

RGB

The RGB color model is based on the way our own eyes work. Light reflected from the outer world enters the eye and strikes the light-sensitive receptors (called cones) on the surface of the retina, at the back of the eyeball. The cones start processing the light information and send it to the brain via the optic nerve. The visual cortex performs more processing, resulting in a perception of the world that gives us the sense that we are "seeing" it. We have three types of cones, each containing one of three photo pigments that are especially sensitive to red, green and blue light. Our eyes use combinations of these three colors to create our perception of all colors.

Additive color

This trichromatic system is called *additive* because the three primary colors of light are added to produce all the other colors, including white. It's puzzling at first, since we know that when primary paint colors are mixed together the result is a muddy brown. But indeed, when red, green and blue lights are overlapped, the result is white light.

The technique of additive color mixing by overlapping red, green and blue light was first developed by Thomas Young (1773–1829), who proposed it as the key to human color vision. This theory of how the eye functions has been extended to the technology of color television and computer color graphics. As with your eye, your scanner and digital camera also use the RGB color model to capture color information. (See "Bringing Images into the Computer" on pages 20–21.) The RGB color information in digital images is stored in three *channels*—one each for red, green and blue—which are combined to produce the composite image. (The channels can be viewed separately in Photoshop using the Channels palette.) Your computer uses RGB to store images and display them on screen. The full spectrum of color we see on a computer monitor or a television screen is actually produced by combinations of red, green and blue light being emitted by the cathode ray tube (or by other means in flat panel display screens).

Subtractive color

In contrast to the light-based RBG models subtractive color models are based on pigments. Most of us are familiar with the color model taught in grade school, in which we mixed paint in the **primary colors** of yellow, red and blue to create the **secondary colors** of orange, green and purple. According to this model, an artist would need only five tubes of paint to create all the colors she wanted: yellow, red and blue (for creating the various *hues* such as yellow-green or reddish-blue) plus black and white for creating tints and shades (such as light yellow-green or dark reddish-blue). This type of color model, in which physical pigments are combined, is called *subtractive* because pigments subtract (absorb) certain colors of light and reflect others. For example, yellow pigments reflect light in the yellow portion of the spectrum and absorb (or subtract) all others.

CMYK

CMYK is a subtractive, pigment-based color model used in the printing industry. Color images such as photos are printed using only four colors of ink (cyan, magenta, yellow and black) to create the various hues and shadings. Traditionally color images are "color separated" by photographing them three times, each time through one of three different color filters in order to create three separate printing plates, one each for cyan, magenta and yellow. (Black is added later.) This is done in a clever way. When an original is photographed through a **red filter**, only the blue and green light pass through. These combine to produce the information needed for the **cyan printing plate**. (So in effect, photographing through a red filter removes the red in the image.) Using a **green filter** removes the green information, leaving the red and blue to produce the **magenta plate**. Finally, using a **blue filter** removes all but the red and green, which combine to produce the **yellow plate**. So cyan, magenta and yellow are called **subtractive primaries** not only because pigments subtract (absorb) color but because each of these three printing plates is created by subtracting one color from the RBG trio. In theory, just these three inks should be enough to faithfully reproduce artwork. But in fact, the blacks they produce are more like muddy browns. So a fourth ink, black, is added to improve shadows and contrast. Today, most color separation is done with computers rather than with filters and cameras. Each color plate is printed as a screen of tiny dots, with yellow printed first, then magenta, then cyan and finally black. These four screens of colored dots overlap to reproduce all the colors in the original image. This is called **four-color process printing** (see "From Photos to Halftone Screens" on page 17.)

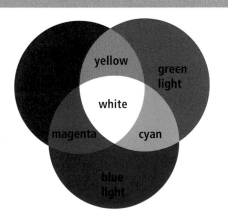

RGB color model, Additive color
The red, green and blue light used by our eyes and by computers combine to produce cyan, magenta and yellow, three of the ink colors used for four-color process printing. When all three RGB lights overlap we see white.

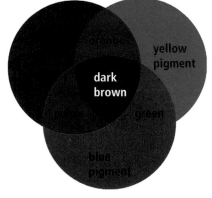

Primary pigment colors, Subtractive color
Red, blue and yellow paints can be mixed to produce the secondary colors of orange, green and purple. When all three primaries are mixed we get a very dark brown.

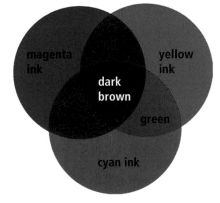

Process ink colors, Subtractive color
When the process colors overlap they produce the same red, green and blue from which they were derived during the color separation process. Printing CMY right on top of each other produces a dark, almost black, brown.

Components of an RGB image

Red

Green

Blue

Composite image

Components of a CMYK image

Yellow

Magenta

Cyan

Black

Converting from RGB to CMYK

So long as an RGB computer image remains only within the RGB computer environment, such as on the Internet, color conversion is not a concern. But in order to print RGB images they must be converted to CMYK, since printers use these four colors of ink to create printed images.

This conversion is done automatically by desktop color printers such as inkjet and color laser printers, so most home and office computer users don't need to be concerned with it. But there are two times when you do need to be concerned: 1). when you're not getting the printed color results you want; and 2.) when you're planning to have your image printed on a conventional four-color printing press.

Improving color on your color printer

The conversion process is not perfect and there are some RGB-specified colors that cannot be printed with CMYK inks. These are called **out-of-gamut** colors because they don't fall within the gamut or range of CMYK-printable colors. (Photoshop includes an alert symbol in its color dialog box which lets you know if any color you've selected is out-of-gamut.) So colors

that look bright and vivid on screen can sometimes look muddy and dull on paper. This is especially true of blue tones. If you're creating computer art from scratch (by painting in Painter, for example), and planning to print it, you may want to work in CMYK mode from the beginning to make sure all the colors you use are within the printing gamut. But if you're editing images that were captured by a scanner or digital camera in RGB mode, you may need to convert at some point. If you're happy with the way an RGB image prints to your color printer, just leave it alone. But if not, follow the guidelines below for converting from RGB to CMYK in Photoshop.

Preparing color images for a printing press

If you plan to send your RGB color images to a service bureau or printer for output for four-color printing, convert them to CMYK, following the guidelines below. But be aware that your images will not always look the same when printed as they do on screen. In fact, because the pure colors of red, green and blue are out-of-gamut, they look less clear and brilliant on these printed pages, after conversion to CMYK, than they did as RGB images on my computer screen.

Guidelines for Converting Digital Images from RGB Mode to CMYK Mode in Photoshop

1. Capture in RGB
Scan your images in RGB mode.

2. Save in RGB
Save in RGB mode and don't convert until you're ready to print since converting back and forth between modes loses some color information each time. Also, RGB images are smaller and will open and save more quickly.

3. Edit in RGB
Do your image-editing and enhancing in RGB mode because some filters and effects only work in this mode.

4. Save a copy in RGB
Save a copy of your RGB image in case you want to go back to do further editing.

5. Preview before converting
Before converting to CMYK, view the RGB images in a second window and chose View > Preview > CMYK to see how the converted image will look. Also choose View > Preview > Gamut Warning to see a version in which any out-of-gamut colors are highlighted.

6. Color correct in RGB
Correct any out-of-gamut colors by using the Hue/Saturation, Levels or Curves controls. Preview again to check your work.

7. Convert to CMYK
Now convert to CMYK and print.

The most powerful weapon of ignorance—the diffusion of printed matter.
—from *War and Peace* by Count Lyof Nikolayevitch Tolstoi (1828–1910)

An honorable profession
The printer has been a respected member of society since the invention of the craft, making it possible for more and me people to have access to books and education. *The Book of Trades*, illustrated by Jost Amman in Germany in 1568, and republished by Dover Publications in 1973, includes the woodcut below and this verse: "The book printer applies the ink, his aide pulls the lever and a sheet is printed; thus many arts become readily accessible; books used to be written by hand." Indeed!

Using Personal Printers

Almost all the projects in this book are made from paper, cloth or other media that's been printed using one of the two most common types of personal printer: a color inkjet printer or a black-and-white laser printer.

Types of printers

INKJET PRINTERS

Inkjet printers print bitmapped images (such as scanned photos) by spraying tiny droplets of ink onto paper, at printer resolutions ranging from 360 dpi to 1440 dpi. They are a great improvement over the previous generation of "dot matrix" printers because they are quieter, able to printer smaller dots for higher print quality and use liquid inks that mix colors better. But inkjet printers can't interpret PostScript language, so they print just the coarse on-screen display of PostScript images and type. To get more accurate PostScript results, it's necessary to buy special software that converts PostScript images into bitmaps and sends that information to the inkjet printer. These include Adobe Type Manager (ATM) for converting fonts and StyleScript (for Mac) or PowerRIP (for Mac or PC) for converting PostScript illustrations and page layouts. You can also use Adobe Acrobat to create a PDF (portable document format) version of a PostScript image and send that to a non-PostScript printer.

LASER PRINTERS

A laser printer uses a rotating disk to reflect laser beams onto the paper. Where the beam touches the paper an electrostatic image area is formed. This attracts electrically-charged toner made of magnetized dry-ink powder that's fixed into place by heat. Laser printers provide printing resolutions ranging from 300 dpi to 1200 dpi, producing very clean, sharp results.

Most laser printers contain PostScript language processors, so they can interpret and accurately print PostScript illustrations and type. Black-and-white PostScript printers cost around $1,000 and are widely used in offices and homes, mostly for printing text. Color PostScript printers are much more expensive and are used primarily by larger businesses.

WHICH TO CHOOSE?

Most of the arts and crafts projects in this book involve printing bitmapped images in color on an inkjet printer. However, the quality of some projects, especially those involving type (such as stationery, for example) will be best if they're printed in PostScript—either on a black-and-white PostScript laser printer or an inkjet printer with a PostScript interpreter. Good-quality color-inkjet printers are inexpensive, with prices starting at $100.

Protecting your printer

Some of the projects in this book will present a challenge to the standard desktop printer, which was designed primarily for printing office documents on plain paper.

IS THE PAPER OR MEDIA APPROPRIATE?

What kinds of media can go through a laser or ink jet printer safely? Paper packages are usually marked with information on what types of printers can handle them. Some can be used only with inkjet printers, some only with laser printers and some with both. When using other types of paper, use common sense and compare it with labeled papers that you know are safe.

IS THE PAPER THE RIGHT THICKNESS?

The manual that came with your printer will tell you the maximum thickness of paper that can pass through it without jamming. Common office "laser paper" is thin enough for both inkjet and laser printers, but card weight (suitable for business cards) is thicker and may cause a laser printer to jam. Use caution when attempting to print on hefty papers of unknown thickness.

WILL PAINTS ON THE PAPER RUB OFF?

What about printing on paper that has paints, inks or other substances already on its surface? Some of the projects in this book involve printing on papers that have been previously decorated with ink or paint using traditional artist tools. So long as the surface is thoroughly dry and fairly flat, it should print without harming your printer. However, some media may interact badly with the chemicals contained in inkjet ink or laser toner. To be absolutely sure, ask the technical staff at the company that makes your printer.

Saving on ink, toner and paper

Printers are relatively inexpensive these days, but the costs of using them can mount up with requirements for toner, ink cartridges and paper. Here are some tips, adapted from Consumer Reports On-Line, to help save money.

- Check your images carefully on-screen before printing on any paper.
- Use draft mode for printing art or photos that are not yet final. This will save on toner and also make printing go faster.
- Don't print photos or other artwork on expensive glossy or other specialty papers until you've proofed them by printing first on cheaper, office paper.
- When printing small images, print more than one to a sheet.

Good fortune to you in the New Year!

Your Digital Toolbox

Essential

To create almost all of the projects in this book you will need the following computer hardware and software:

- a Macintosh or a PC running Windows
- Photoshop or other "image-editing" application
- a flatbed scanner
- a color inkjet printer

Optional

The following are optional, but will enable you to create all of the projects in this book:

- Adobe Illustrator or another PostScript illustration program
- Adobe PageMaker or Adobe InDesign; or QuarkXpress
- a basic set of PostScript fonts
- a digital camera
- a high-resolution, black-and-white laser printer

(Also see the traditional artist tools and materials listed under "Your Basic Art Kit" on page 77.)

Taking chances

I try to be careful about what kind of paper I put through my printers. But sometimes I take chances because a paper is too pretty to resist. To create a Chinese New Year's greeting, I used my laser printer to print in black on a 5-inch by 6-inch piece of decorated "Joss paper" from San Francisco's Chinatown. I discovered that the black toner did not adhere well to the metallic stamping in the center of the paper, so I moved my message to the top and bottom of the page.

2 Working with Photos and Scans

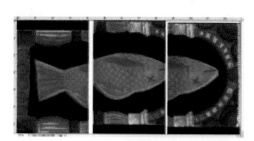

O YOU REMEMBER THE EARLY DAYS of personal computing—only about fifteen years ago—when people used programs such as MacPaint to fill squares and ovals with ready-made wicker texture? Computer drawing and painting have come a long way since then. The first desktop graphics programs are now in their sixth or even tenth versions and computer-made illustrations are seen everywhere, from advertising to fine arts. In this chapter you'll discover how to create digital images—either from scratch or by scanning photos and art—and learn how image-editing programs can be used to edit digital images so that they look *better* (good color and focus) or *different* (special filter effects, color distortions and so on).

Scanning Traditional Art and Photos

The most common way of creating art on a computer is by starting with a scan (either one you do yourself or one that's pre-scanned on a CD-ROM disk that you buy) and working with it either in a painting program or a drawing program. It may be as simple as a rough pencil sketch that you use as a drawing guide, or as complex as a series of full-color photographs that you alter and combine into a montage.

Scanning traditional art work

Any piece of flat or thin art that's small enough to fit on a scanner bed can be scanned and imported into a painting or drawing program. For art that's larger,

Scanning oversize art

This drawing, made by my son Rufus Ashford, was done with oil pastel on 12-inch by 18-inch paper. The piece was too large to scan in one pass on my scanner, which has an image area of 8 ³/4 inches by 14 inches. So I scanned the drawing in three sections and assembled them in Photoshop. To do this, I pasted each section into its own layer in one large document, so that I could move each one until they overlapped correctly. Then, to disguise the seams, I selected the edge of each overlapping section, applied a feather, and deleted it. The reassembled image was then rotated to its correct vertical orientation.

Making it better

The red background in my violin painting was too detailed and garish. To fix it digitally, I scanned the painting and used Photoshop to select the background, lighten it and reduce its contrast. I also added magenta to the yellows in the violin to make them blend better with the browns and applied a filter to soften the overall texture. More details on this type of editing are found in "Basics of Image Editing" on page 31.

thicker or three-dimensional, there are two options: 1) oversized art can be scanned in sections and reassembled in Photoshop or another image-editing program; or 2) larger paintings and sculptures can be photographed, either with a digital camera or with a conventional camera that produces prints that can be scanned.

SCANNING YOUR BEST ART

Digital images of your own best art can be used to promote your work, either on the Internet or on printed pieces such as flyers and brochures. You can also edit your scanned work to experiment with variations in color, composition or textural effects, without affecting the original. In addition, you can use sections of your art (either altered or unaltered) as textures or graphic elements for other uses. For example, a corner of a watercolor containing flowers could be printed and used as gift wrap.

USING YOUR NOT-SO-GOOD ART

Drawings and paintings that contain slips of the pen or other mistakes can be fixed digitally to some extent by scanning them and altering the scan. The original will remain the same, of course, but the edited scan can be printed on watercolor paper, for example, and framed as a finished piece. In addition, nicely rendered sections of an otherwise unsatisfactory piece can be scanned and used in other projects. Such "passages" can be used for other purposes, for example, as background textures for a digital collage.

Scanning photographs

Photographs are one of the most important sources of visual information in our culture. They can be used simply as photo images, but they also make it possible to bring a wealth of physical detail into computer illustrations. In addition, scanned photographs can be edited and combined to create new works of art. (For more information on cameras and photography, see "Bringing Images into the Computer" on page 20).

BUILDING A PERSONAL PHOTO LIBRARY

I've enjoyed photography since my first experiences with a box camera and home darkroom back in the late 1960s. Over the years I've taken many photographs and now have a personal library of hundreds of them. I try to take my camera with me whenever I visit a new or interesting place and I advise you to do the same. You'll soon have a collection of copyright-free images.

COLLECTING PHOTO "SWIPES"

I also like to collect interesting photographs from posters, calendars and magazines. These "swipes" inspire me with ideas for my own photos and I sometimes use them as references for drawing (see "Tracing Over Photo References" on page 29). Photographs taken by other people are copyrighted images however and cannot be used directly without permission (see "Understanding Copyright" on page 30).

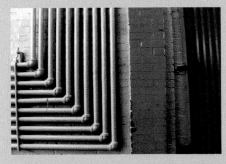

Photos opportunities everywhere!
For the past 30 years, I've carried a 35mm camera with me whenever I go on vacation or visit an interesting place and I often snap pictures around my own town, house and yard when the light, the season or the weather conditions are photogenic. As a result, I've amassed a collection of hundreds of original photographs of people, animals, gardens, outdoor scenes, buildings, cityscapes and still-life scenes. I use these photos in my graphic-design books and as raw materials for art projects, as well as to record my life and family events. The old buildings above are at the desert gold-mining ghost town of Calico, California. The exotic fish was photographed at the Scripps Aquarium in La Jolla, California. The painted brick wall with pipes was taken at a printing press in an older factory building in Tennessee.

Digital Drawing and Painting

In addition to scanning traditional art and photos, it's possible to create original art on a computer by "painting" (with a program that works with bitmapped images), or by "drawing" (with a program that works with shapes, lines and curves). Painting is best for creating traditional-looking, textured work, while drawing is best for crisp, hard-edged styles. (The differences between painting and drawing programs are explained in Chapter 1. To review, see "Understanding Bitmaps and PostScript" on page 10 and "Choosing Software for Graphics" on pages 12–13.)

Drawing and painting original digital art

From scan to art
To create the clean-edged, poster-like art below, I scanned a photo of a koi pond taken at the Self-Realization Fellowship Gardens in Encinitas, California, imported it into Adobe Illustrator and drew shapes over it with the pen tool (below). To create a more painterly illustration, I used Corel Painter (bottom). For details, see "Tracing Over Photo References" on page 29.

Drawing and painting original art with a computer is different from using traditional tools for at least two reasons. First, moving a mouse (or even a special drawing stylus) across a pad is not as immediate and "tactile" as moving a pencil across a paper. There is a physical and psychological distance between what our hand is doing and what our eye is seeing on the screen. Secondly, the digital space in which computer images are created is not as complex and highly textured as real paints and papers are. So digital images made "from scratch" can sometimes be too simple to satisfy us. It's often helpful—even crucial—to bring scanned images into a computer painting or drawing, either as textural elements or parts of a montage, or as templates used to guide our drawing.

WORKING WITH A PAINT PROGRAM

In the early days of computer art, programs such as MacPaint were used to make simple, digital paintings using a limited palette of tools. Artists and software developers soon exhausted the potential of these programs and came to realize that digital editing of scanned images held more promise.

IMAGE-EDITING PROGRAMS

The development of Adobe Photoshop has revolutionized both photography and digital art-making. Photoshop makes it possible for artists to bring the richly textured details of the outside world (via scans of photos and other art work) into the computer environment and then work with them to correct or alter their color, focus, composition and so on. (An analogous development took place in the world of music as musicians and developers heard the harsh and limited timbres produced by synthesizers and moved toward keyboards that use sampled sound—based on recordings of traditional instruments and voices—instead of electronically generated tones.) It still is possible to paint from scratch using a "paint" program such as Photoshop but professional illustrators rarely create images this way. Ten years ago I discovered that most computer artists "start with a scan." My book of the

"Tracing" over Photo References

Artists have used photographs as drawing aids ever since photography was invented, although they're sometimes reluctant to admit it. In fact, the great French painter Ingres (1780–1867) lived just long enough to see the first photographs and commented: "Which of us could achieve this exactitude … this delicate modeling … indeed, what a wonderful thing photography is—but one dare not say that aloud." When I first began painting, back in the early 1970s, I often used photographs as sources, laboriously transferring their lines and curves to canvas using a grid system. The computer makes it much easier to use photos as a visual reference by making it possible to import a scanned photo into a drawing or painting program and "trace" on top of it. I advise you to take advantage of this powerful tool. As the cartoonist Robert Crumb said, "You say you can't draw a straight line? Don't let those artists fool you; they all use rulers!"

Using photos as drawing references
Any scanned photo can be opened in a bitmapped program such as Photoshop or Painter (where it can be edited) or imported into a drawing program such as Illustrator or FreeHand (where it cannot be edited, but can be seen, changed in size and positioned). In Photoshop and Painter a photo can be placed in a separate layer and then you can draw on top of it in another layer. Likewise, in Illustrator or FreeHand, you can import a photo and draw on top of it, using it as a guide. In both cases, the photo itself remains unaltered. The process is like placing tracing paper over a photo, except that in the computer the tracing paper is perfectly transparent. You can trace over as much or as little of a photo as you like, and you can combine elements from several different photos.

Preparing photos for tracing
Sometimes it's a good idea to edit a photo before using it as a drawing reference in order to make it easier to see essential elements. For example, you may want to increase the contrast or apply a filter that exaggerates the borders between light and dark areas. It may also help to simplify things visually by converting a color photo to black-and-white. (For more information on this kind of editing see "Basics of Image Editing" on page 31.)

Using sketches
Rough sketches done in pencil or crayon can also be scanned and used as templates in both painting and drawing programs. This technique makes it possible to doodle and play with familiar hand tools until a visual idea looks right and then use the computer to complete the image with more carefully drawn elements. You can also use real tracing paper to trace over a photograph, then scan your tracing and import it into a drawing or painting program to use as a template. (See "Evolution of a greeting card" on page 80 for an example of this technique.)

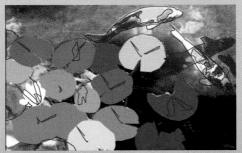

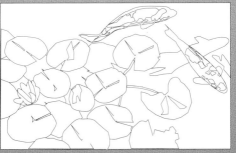

Tracing over an imported a photo
To create the clean-edged, poster-like koi art on the previous page, I scanned my koi photo and imported it into Adobe Illustrator. I used the pen tool, driven by the mouse, to draw around the shapes of fish and lily leaves, using a stroke of red and no color fill (a fill of None) so that it would be easy for me to see my work.

Adding color
Using Illustrator's eyedropper tool, I was able to sample colors from the imported photo and use them to fill the shapes I had drawn. Many other programs, including Photoshop and Painter, make it possible to specify colors by sampling them directly from scanned photos.

Finishing the drawing
After all the shapes had been filled with color, I removed the red outlines by specifying a stroke of None for all the shapes. After viewing the colored art, I decided to add one gradient fill to make the gold background rectangle more interesting. The gradient is a blend between the gold color at the top of the photo and the dark blue at the bottom. See the previous page for the result.

Converting to black-and-white
Once the koi art was finished, I saved another copy and converted all the shapes to a fill of white and a stroke of black. This had the effect of creating an image that looks like a black-and-white line drawing. I opened this Illustrator EPS art in Photoshop in order to convert it to TIFF format, so that I could use it for a bitmapped painting treatment.

Painting in Painter
To create a more painterly illustration, I imported my black-and-white Illustrator drawing into Corel Painter and painted directly onto it using a Wacom tablet and stylus. I used the Artist Pastel Chalk tool to add the color (again, sampling from the scanned photo, which I also imported and had on-screen at the same time), emphasized the outlines using a black Charcoal tool, then used the Smear tool to blend the color areas.

FIND IT IN *START WITH A SCAN*
For more detailed information on using photographs as drawing aides see "Working from Photo References" on pages 48–52 in *Start with a Scan: A Guide to Transforming Scanned Photos and Objects into High-Quality Art*, 2nd edition, Janet Ashford and John Odam (Peachpit Press, 2000).

Comparing Mucha's design with the photos from which he worked gives us useful insight into the artistic process. It is clear that no photograph was ever slavishly copied; it represented only a point of departure from which inspiration takes over. With his meticulous attention to detail, Mucha certainly used the pictures to check things such as the precise position of fingers on a hand holding something— often a stumbling block for even otherwise competent artists —as well as for a correct perspective and relations between people and objects. Beyond that, the heart of every design is an expression of the artist's soul.

—Jack Rennert, "Mucha and Photography,"
The Artist and the Camera: Degas to Picasso
(edited by Dorothy Kosinski, Dallas Museum
of Art/Yale University Press, 1999)

same name grew out of this experience. Photoshop currently sells for around $600, but a new version for home users, Photoshop Elements, sells for around $100 and contains most of the features that crafters need.

USING PAINTER

Another direction was taken by the developers of Painter, originally created by Fractal Design in 1991 and now owned by Corel. The tools in Painter are designed to imitate the look of "natural media" and do a delightfully good job of reproducing the textural strokes made by tools such as charcoal, pastels, watercolors and oils. Using Painter means having almost the entire contents of an art supply store at your disposal, without any mess or clean-up.

USING A POSTSCRIPT PROGRAM

PostScript drawing programs such as Illustrator, FreeHand and CorelDRAW were originally developed as aids for mechanical illustration and are still widely used to create technical drawings as well as slick, sophisticated illustrations. The main feature of these programs is their ability to easily create and manipulate geometrical shapes, so the issues of hand-drawing versus computer-drawing are not as relevant. Drawing programs are often used to create patterns because of their ability to "transform" shapes through scaling, rotating, flipping, copying and offsetting, skewing and so on. But again, recognizing the limitations of the "from scratch" approach, PostScript illustration programs are designed to import scanned images for use as "templates" or drawing guides. These images appear in a background layer and can be seen on-screen as we draw over them, but don't appear in the finished art.

Understanding Copyright

Copyright laws are designed to protect the work of artists, writers and other creators so that no one else can use and profit from their work without getting permission. Creative work is automatically covered by copyright protection, whether or not it has been registered with the copyright office or includes a copyright notice. However, registering and including the notice make it easier to prove who the copyright holder is.

Books that are at least 75 years old are generally in the *public domain*, which means that the original copyright has expired. Art from these books can be scanned and used without permission. (The decorative initial shown here was scanned from a 1922 issue of an arts magazine published by Condé Nast.) Artwork

in books and magazines that are less than 75 years old is copyrighted and cannot be used without permission. In addition, most decorative papers, including marbled papers and wrapping paper are copyrighted designs.

I keep a file of interesting clipped-out photos, pages and paper on hand, both for inspiration and to use as drawing aids. But I don't use scans of these images in a published work without obtaining permission (unless I've altered them so much that they're no longer recognizable, or if I've used only a very small, unrecognizable portion). I use my best judgment, bearing in mind how I would want my own published work to be treated.

Basics of Image Editing

Image editing is the process of improving or altering digital images. Most of the photos we see in books and magazines today have been scanned and edited in some way, especially to improve their composition, contrast, focus and color. I've used one of my own photos (a street scene near Lake Garda in Italy) as an example of how a photo with various problems can be "fixed." The same techniques can be applied to scans of traditional artwork and to scans of real objects (see pages 32–33). I used Photoshop because it's considered to be the best image-editor. It's available for both Macs and PCs, in a full-featured version and a lower priced version called Photoshop Elements. Other less expensive image-editing programs also provide functions for cropping, sharpening and adjusting contrast. If you're not using Photoshop, explore your own program to see what similar functions it has.

Four basic steps for improving less-than-good photos

I used the following four-step procedure to improve the appearance of my original Italian street scene photo (above), which was marred by poor composition, low contrast and washed-out color. These four steps will work well to improve most scanned photos.

1. Crop, unclutter and sharpen

Using Photoshop, I cropped the photo to remove the plastic cover in the lower right-hand corner and the white sky in the upper left-hand corner. I then used the rubber stamp tool to paint out the distracting pipes along the building at the upper left, by sampling sections of the adjacent sky. My aim was to remove distracting elements and tighten the composition of the photo. I then applied the Unsharp Mask filter to sharpen the focus of the entire image.

2. Increase contrast

My photo was taken on a rainy, overcast day and I was pointing my camera slightly toward the sky, so the colors were washed out and the image lacked contrast. To improve this, I used Levels to increase contrast by increasing the blackness of the blacks. (It's usually also a good idea to increase the whiteness of the whites in an image, but in this photo the light areas were already light enough.)

3. Lighten muddy midtones

Midtones are the gray areas in the middle ranges between black and white. Darkening the blacks made some of these areas too dark, especially in the doorways at the bottom of the street, so I used Levels again to lighten the midtones slightly.

4. Increase saturation

The contrast and clarity of the image was now greatly improved but it still looked pale, so I used the Hue/Saturation controls to increase the color saturation, restoring the brightly painted walls of the buildings. Now the image looks more like what my eyes saw on that day, rather than what the camera recorded.

1

2

3

4

Tips for Scanning Objects

Stay in focus
To get good focus, scan objects that are fairly thin, such as leaves, pressed flowers or small sea shells. Objects that are thicker or have protruding parts will be in focus near the scanner glass but less focussed further away. In general, a scanner can focus on items that are within about 1 inch of the glass.

Handle large objects
A large object, such as a doll or stuffed animal, can be scanned in sections and reassembled in an image-editing program, just as with oversized art work (see page 26).

Contain unwieldy objects
Objects that are round will need to be corralled with small pieces of cardboard or rulers or books. Also, you can build small supports from cardboard or foam core board to keep unbalanced objects from toppling over.

Keep your scanner clean
Be careful about scanning items that are wet (such as a slice of orange) or that contain a lot of dust or chaff (such as dry beans or pasta). Be ready to clean your scanner glass with window cleaner and a soft cloth and keep a can of aerosol "air" on hand to blow away specks of dust. Sometimes it's possible to get good results by placing wet or dusty items in a plastic freezer bag or on a sheet of acetate.

Create new shadows
The shadows cast in the scanning process are not natural-looking and can be removed by silhouetting (see page 36). Photoshop makes it possible to add a soft-edged drop shadow to silhouetted objects. When printed, they'll look as though they're actually resting on the page.

Use the right background
Scanning real objects may mean that you can't put the scanner lid down. I keep two large pieces of paper handy near my scanner—one white and one black—to place over objects. I use white if I want to use the shadow cast by the scanner. But if I'm planning to silhouette the object, I've found that a black background is easiest to select and remove.

Illuminate transparent objects
When scanning objects made of glass, it's sometimes helpful to shine a desklight at the object, aiming the light from the side to keep the light itself from also being scanned!

Scanning Real Objects

Scanning real objects opens up a fascinating world of images. Small, lightweight items can be place directly on a scanner, bypassing the camera and making it possible to capture images immediately. But since scanners were designed for scanning flat, clean pieces of paper, it's good to follow a few guidelines (see "Tips for Scanning Objects" at the left).

Scanning single objects
A scanner can be used to capture a "portrait" of any small item, providing either an instant illustration or an image to be used for further manipulation.

Scanning multiple objects
By covering your scanner with a bunch of small objects, you can create an interesting illustration or background texture. Likely objects include small toys, marbles, game pieces, playing cards, dry pasta or beans, flowers, leaves, popcorn, paper clips or other office supplies and so on.

Scanning textured objects
It's possible to create many interesting background textures by scanning objects such as cloth, baskets, pieces of wood, rocks, samples of marble or textured paper. You can zero in on the object and crop away its rough edges in order to get a texture that fills your whole rectangular image area.

Bypassing the Camera

Your home and workplace are filled with small objects that can be scanned. Objects can be scanned alone, in groups, in small "still life" arrangements" or you can zero in on interesting textures. Here are just a few ideas:

Clothing items
buttons
braid, trim, rickrack
jewelry
hats and purses
scarves and shawls
textured cloth
yarn and thread

Food
chips and snacks
beans and pasta
decorative gourds
jelly beans
Indian corn
popcorn and pretzels

Tools and hardware
screwdrivers
wrenches
clamps
gears
nails and screws
wire

Tatting design

Plastic checker

Redwood leaf

Small plastic toys

Straw hat brim

Household items
baskets
dishes
egg crates
kitchen utensils
matches
potpourri
trivets
graters

Vegetable pasta

Mexican blanket

Toys
alphabet blocks
dolls
game pieces
marbles
puppets
kites

Office supplies
paper clips
pens and pencils
rubber bands
seals and stamps

Natural materials
seashells
rocks and stones
bark
feathers
flowers
leaves

Using Copyright-Free Clip Art

An easy and flexible way to bring images into the computer is by scanning *clip art*—art and illustration that's copyright-free and intended to be "clipped" from a book. Clip art, especially from historical sources, is a rich fund of ideas and images for craft work and illustration, putting us in touch with the handiwork of our ancestors and kindred crafters from around the world. I came upon my first book of historical clip art back in 1973 and I've been hooked ever since.

Finding printed clip art

Copyright-free art can be scanned from two main sources: clip art books and old books with expired copyrights.

BOOKS OF PRINTED CLIP ART

Many publishers produce books of "scan-able" clip art. My favorite is the Dover Pictorial Archive with over 600 books of royalty-free images that can be used without special permission. Most of the art is charming and well-rendered European and American engravings and woodcuts from books published from the 1500s to the early 1900s. Dover Publication's books are well-designed, cleanly printed and cheap. Dover also publishes fascinating books of full-color historical illustration and ornament. I cannot recommend Dover's books highly enough, both as sources of images for craft and design and as an introduction to the range of beautiful printed ornament and illustration produced during the past 500 years.

Other companies also produce excellent printed clip art. Stemmer House has about 80 books of black-and-white folk art designs from Asia, the near East, Native America, Africa, and Latin America, as well as Medieval Europe and Early America. Art Direction Book Company publishes American advertising clip art from the 1930s, 40s and 50s.

FIND IT IN *START WITH A SCAN*
Editing scanned clip art
For more detailed information on editing scanned clip art, adding color and other techniques see Chapter 5, "Working with Printed Clip Art," pages 25–46 in *Start with a Scan* (Peachpit Press, 2000).
Converting scans to PostScript
Scanned drawings that are fairly simple can also be converted to PostScript format using Adobe Streamline, a program that traces around shapes to produce PostScript outlines. For more information see "Converting Bitmaps to PostScript Art" on pages 36–43 in *Start with a Scan* (Peachpit Press, 2000).

Painting color into black-and-white art
I scanned a line drawing of a Pa Ndau textile design from the Hmong people of Southeast Asia from *Hmong Textile Designs* (Stemmer House, 1990). I added color by using the paint bucket tool in Photoshop to dump bright solid color into the white spaces in the design. To create a version that looks more like the actual hand-appliqued fabric made by Hmong women, I dumped black paint into the primary shapes, so that the black outlines were in effect removed. Then I added pink to the black areas and blue to the white areas so that the design contains only solid color areas with no black outlines.

CLIP ART ON CD-ROM

Direct Imagination produces CD-ROM collections of luscious decorative art from Europe and Asia, including a complete digital reproduction of Owen Jones 1856 classic, *The Grammar of Ornament*. Dover has also introduced clip art on CD-ROM—about 26 sets so far in both black-and-white and color. (See the Resources section for more information on ordering clip art.)

Editing clip art

Clip art can be captured, edited and used in a variety of ways. Most black-and-white clip art is available in printed books and can be scanned simply by placing the book page on the scanner. Once it's scanned, you can alter the design and add color.

COLORING BLACK-AND-WHITE ART

Scanned art can be colored in Photoshop or Painter either by coloring the solid black or white areas or by painting with semitransparent paint that allows the line work to show through.

EDITING COLOR CLIP ART

Clip art that is already in color can be used as-is or can be edited to create a more pleasing palette or to match colors you want for a particular project. Scanned color art can be edited in Photoshop using any of the techniques described in "Basics of Image Editing" on page 31 or with silhouetting, drop shadowing, posterization, solarization and filtering, as described on pages 36–39. PostScript color art can be edited in programs such as Illustrator, FreeHand or CorelDRAW. Art in EPS format can also be converted to a bitmap by opening it in Photoshop. Once converted, it can be edited in the same way as any bitmap. (For information on the difference see "Understanding Bitmaps and PostScript on page 10.)

Tips for Scanning Black-and-White Clip Art

• Place a piece of black paper behind the page you wish to scan to reduce show-through of printing from the other side of the page.

• Spread the book open and place the page you want to scan face down on your scanner glass. Weight down the book with something heavy (such as a dictionary) if necessary, to keep the page flat against the glass.

• Scan in grayscale mode, rather than bitmap mode, to capture the most detail.

• When scanning engravings with very fine lines, use a higher than usual resolution to capture the most detail.

Adding a color layer
To duplicate the look of a hand-colored engraving, I opened a scan of a black-and-white engraving in Photoshop and created a new layer above it in which I painted areas of color. I blended the color layer with the engraving using Multiply mode to make the color look as though it is behind the black lines and also tried Overlay mode, which created the effect of adding color to the black lines themselves (large figure at right). (This violinist was scanned from *Women: A Pictorial Archive from Nineteenth-Century Sources*, Dover Publications, 1978.)

Altering and Combining Images

An image-editing program such as Photoshop makes it possible to make scanned photos and other images look *better* (see "Basics of Image Editing" on page 31) and also to make images look *different* in various ways. A good program provides many of the same special effects that darkroom photographers have used for years, such as *dodge and burn* (to lighten or darken areas of a photo), posterization and color filters. In addition to these effects, image-editors also make it possible to "cut out" parts of an image, just as though you were using scissors. This "selection" can then be edited separately and can be copied and pasted into other images. All in all, it's worthwhile to become familiar with all the functions of your image-editor, as they greatly expand the range of your creativity in working with photos and other scanned images.

Working with "selections"

Being able to outline part of an image to create a "selection" is one of the most powerful tools provided by an image-editor. It makes it possible to remove unwanted backgrounds or to make them less obtrusive by editing them to reduce color or contrast. When a background is removed entirely, the remaining foreground elements are silhouetted and can be copied and pasted into other images as separate elements. Silhouetted figures can also be used alone and look especially effective when floated over a soft drop shadow.

Creating selections

Working with a photo of my friend Tom, I used the lasso and wand tools in Photoshop to select him so that I could edit him separately from the background. I could easily choose the "Inverse" command to also select the background (that is, everything except Tom). When viewed in a separate "channel" in Photoshop, selection areas appear white on a black background. Areas that are white can be edited, while areas that are black will be protected from editing whenever the selection is active. Above are the channels for Tom (left) and for the background (right).

Using selections to alter and to silhouette

To make Tom's office background less distracting (and to make the figure pop forward) I loaded the background channel as a selection and used the Hue/Saturation controls to remove all the color saturation from this area, in effect converting the background to black-and-white. As a variation, I also created a silhouette of Tom by removing the background entirely. I added a soft drop shadow behind the figure.

Adding, removing and "rubber stamping" elements

Once you have silhouetted an object, it's possible to play tricks with it, such as pasting it into a completely different photograph. (This works best if the two photos have similar lighting conditions and shadows that fall in the same direction). Once you start to play around with image editing you'll realize why photographs can no longer be used as documentary evidence.

Playing with reality
I decided that Tom might enjoy playing accordion in the woods out back, instead of in the office. So I scanned another photo of my daughter and a friend in the backyard (left) and copied and pasted the figure of Tom into the new photo (right).

Rubber stamping to remove elements
I then used Photoshop's rubber stamp tool to sample areas of the trees and foliage to use in painting out the figures of Florrie and Maria, leaving Tom alone in the woods (far left). Because his image was on a separate layer, I could easily paint out the young women without disturbing Tom.

Matching color, softening edges
Because Tom was photographed under incandescent lighting, his warm yellow color cast didn't match the cooler, bluer outdoor lighting of the woods. So I used Image>Adjust>Variations to add a yellow cast to the background, making it look more harmonious with the warm tones on Tom. I also applied a slight blur to the edges of Tom so that he blended better with the scene, instead of looking like a cutout. Over all, the finished image looks remarkably like a real photograph.

We have our brush and colors—paint Paradise and in we go.
—Nikos Kazantzakis

FIND IT IN START WITH A SCAN
For more detailed information on using Photoshop to make selections, create silhouettes and delete unwanted elements, see "Crafting Quality Images" starting on page 21 of *Start with a Scan*, 2nd edition (Peachpit Press, 2000).

Applying Special Effects

Contrast, posterization and solarization

Photoshop, along with other image-image programs, includes commands that automatically apply effects to images. These can be used to make scanned photographs look more interesting or more like "graphics" than photos. Three of the most common effects are high contrast, posterization and solarization.

Creating a high-contrast image

Most image-editing programs include tools for increasing contrast. Photoshop's Levels controls can also be used to make blacks blacker and whites whiter, but with more control than is usually provided by Contrast functions. I used Levels to create a high contrast version of my photo of a sail boat on Morro Bay, California. Cropping to a horizontal format also made the image more dramatic.

Creating a posterization

Photoshop's posterization function imitates the traditional darkroom technique in which filters are used to reduce an image to a smaller number of tonal levels. I used Photoshop to apply a four-level posterization to a photo of spiraling succulents, tended by horticulturist Jaen Treesinger at the Cafe Beaujolais in Mendocino. The technique works well with this image, which already contains fairly smooth and simple color areas.

Creating a solarization

Another traditional darkroom technique is "solarization," in which filters are used to convert some of the tones in an image to their color opposites. Applying solarization to my photo of birthday party cupcakes makes the scene look even more festive and whimsical.

Using filters

In computer graphics, "filters" are ready-made sets of calculations designed to alter images in specific ways, often in order to imitate the look of various kinds of natural techniques, such as drawing with pencil or painting. Using filters is as simple as selecting the image—or a portion of it—and then choosing the desired filter from a menu list. Photoshop provides over 120 built-in filters that imitate traditional artistic effects and also that blur, sharpen, distort, create textures and so on. Many so-called "third party" companies also provide "plug-in" filters than can be used with

Photoshop and other image-editing programs. See the Resources section for a listing of third-party filter suppliers.

One may do whate'er one likes
In Art: the only thing is, to
make sure
That one does like it.
—Robert Browning (1812–1889)

Creating filter effects

I applied just four of Photoshop's many graphic filters in order to change my photo of a San Francisco Victorian house into an "illustration." For more demonstrations of the use of filters see "Using Filters on Line Art," page 35, "Using Filters on Scanned Objects," pages 70-71, and "Applying Graphic Filters to Photos," pages 92–93 of *Start with a Scan* (Peachpit Press, 2000). Also see *The Photoshop 6 Wow! Book* by Linnea Dayton and Jack Davis (Peachpit Press, 2002).

Filter>Stylize>Find edges

Filter>Distort>Shear

Filter>Artistic>Cutout

Filter>Artistic>Colored pencil

Working with Old Photos

I have a folder full of old family photos which my two grandmothers, Florence Scriven Munro and Jean Chisholm Isaacs, copied for all their grandchildren. Perhaps you have a similar collection of treasures. Many of my photos were taken around the turn of the last century and have been marred by cracks and chipped emulsion. Fixing the flaws in old photos used to be something done laboriously in the darkroom. But now personal computers make it possible for amateurs to rescue family photos rather easily by scanning them and using image-editing programs such as Photoshop to apply touch-ups and repairs.

Restoring damaged photos

Photoshop's "rubber stamp" tool is an especially powerful assistant for restoring old photos, for it can be used to pick up samples from undamaged areas of an image and use this "paint" to brush out adjacent cracks and spots. (See page 37 for another use of the rubber stamp tool—removing unwanted objects.)

Coloring black-and-white photos

Scans of black-and-white photos can be easily converted to brown-and-white images that mimic the soft, nineteenth century look of sepia prints. In addition, image-editing tools can be used to add color tints to areas of a photo (eyes, lips, cheeks and so on) in the same way that monochrome photos used to be hand-tinted with paints, before the availability of color photography.

Restoring a damaged photo
The lovely studio portrait above was taken around 1915 and includes four generations of my family: my paternal grandmother, her first child (my father's older brother), her father, and her father's mother. But a close-up of my grandmother shows that the photo is marred by many white spots where the surface has chipped away, as well as dirt and some fine line cracks.

Cloning and adding an overall color
I scanned the photo into Photoshop and used the rubber stamp tool to sample areas of skin and hair and used them to paint out the various dark and light splotches on the photo. I then used the Hue/Saturation controls to colorize the photo and add a soft brown hue that makes the image look like an old-style sepia photo.

Adding color tints
Next I used the brush tool in Photoshop to paint blues, pinks and yellows onto a separate layer above that of the photo. It set the layer to Soft Light blending mode so that the colors blend very softly with that of the sepia-tone image. This process added subtle color highlights to my grandmother's eyes, cheeks, mouth, hair and dress.

Playing with the Past

I love the dignity and reserve of old photo studio portraits. In the early part of the twentith century photography was mostly in the hands of professionals. Having a family photograph taken was a special and sometimes solemn occasion, marked by expense and planning in advance. The long exposure times meant that subjects had to sit still for fairly long periods and smiling seemed to be discouraged. It was only later, with the advent of cheap cameras for the masses, that we see the informality, spontaneity and amateurish composition that marks "snapshots." But the seriousness of old photos seems to cry out for some tampering, since these images from another time provide a natural foil for digital flights of fancy in color, collage and filtering. Here are some examples of my own "playing with the past."

Wild and crazy Grandma

My father's mother was a devout and hard-working woman who supported her three sons by herself when her husband died in 1929. She eventually moved her family from Pittsburgh to Los Angeles in the early 1940s and enjoyed a long career as a first grade teacher at a Baptist church school. She enjoyed children and holidays and was always kind and loving to me and my brother as we were growing up. Perhaps she would have enjoyed this colorful rendering of her photo. In Photoshop I colored the original portrait blue and then drew shapes in various colors into three different layers above the one containing the photo. These layers were blended using different blending modes.

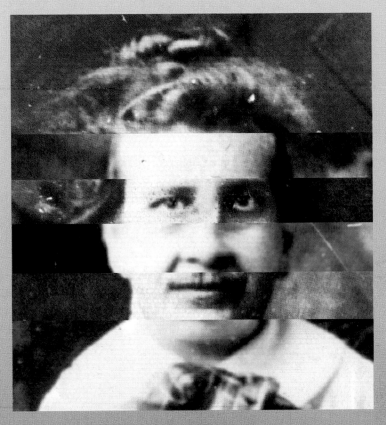

Gene splicing

The four family members in the portrait on page 40 share facial similarities, so I thought it would be interesting to shuffle them around. I scanned a close-up of each person in the original photo and placed each one in a separate layer in Photoshop, lining them up so their features overlapped. Then I used Hue/Saturation to apply a different color tint to each person and deleted sections of each to create a strip effect. Visible now are my grandmother's hair and eyes, her father's forehead and mouth, her grandmother's nose, and her son's chin and shoulders.

Creating a sense of depth

Placing collage elements in different layers helps to create a sense of depth. This can be enhanced by making background layers lighter, less contrasty or less focused. Drop shadows, such as the one behind the sheet music above, can be added to make elements look as though they are actually pieces of cut paper resting on a page.

Assembling family images

To create a collage in memory of my maternal grandfather, James Munro, I scanned family photos and a page from the family bible recording my grandfather's birth in 1887. To express the theme of his childhood in Scotland and later life in California, I scanned the Munro tartan from *Scottish Tartans in Full Color* (Dover, 1992), an ad for Scotland from *Travel and Vacation Advertising Cuts from the Twenties and Thirties* (Dover, 1994) and a sheet music cover, loaned to me by Vykki Mende Gray and David Swarens, collectors in San Diego. I also painted over the images with yellow and pink. Photoshop's layering and transparency functions made it possible to combine all these elements into a subtle and well-blended final image (opposite page). In addition, digital collage makes it possible to create any number of variations using the same materials (left).

"Painting" on scanned images

Digital collage also makes it easy to paint on top of scanned elements, without fear of permanently marking them. Painting can be done in a layer above the one containing the image to be embellished or can be done to a copy of the image, so that the original scan is unchanged. I painted with yellow in a layer above my grandfather's photo, then blended this layer using the Multiply mode.

Digital Collage and Photomontage

Collage is the art of choosing, cutting, arranging and pasting images from various sources to create a new piece of art. The name is derived from the French verb *coller*, "to glue." The practice began in 1912 when the Cubist artists Pablo Picasso and Georges Braque glued bits of newspaper clippings, wallpaper, playing cards, wrapping paper and cigarette wrappers onto their paintings. Other European artists, especially of the Dada and Surrealist movements, went on to use cut paper scraps to create images that were fantastic or absurd. As Jim Harter wrote: "Drawing upon such intellectual energies of the day as Freud's theories and Jung's concept of the collective unconscious, and reflecting the rapidly growing threat of domination of man by the machine, the strongly symbolic visual language of collage was transferred into a vital medium for serious social and personal statement." (*Harter's Picture Archive for Collage and Illustration*, Dover, 1978.) The art of collage eventually led to photo montage, the technique of arranging and juxtaposing photos and other printed reproductions.

The power of layering

Traditional collage and montage require hours of laborious cutting and pasting. Digital collage also requires some degree of painstaking silhouetting if you want to remove an element from its background (see "Altering and Combining Images" on page 36). But once each element of a collage has been placed in its own layer—in a program such as Photoshop or Illustrator—the different elements can be arranged and rearranged endlessly without the mess or finality of glue. Also, elements can be re-sized, rotated, flipped, skewed, colored, reversed to negative, filtered, painted over and decorated. In addition, images in a digital collage can be made transparent (ranging from 1 percent to 99 percent opaque) and can be blended with each other using a variety of blending modes that imitate darkroom techniques.

Family Bible page,
Normal, 68%

Sepia page section,
Multiply, 65%

Munro tartan,
Normal, 57%

Munro family 1927
Normal, 64%

Grandparents 1949
Normal, 76%

Little Janet
Normal, 100%

Bible page ornament
Normal, 67%

Pink outline
Normal, 39%

Yellow highlight
Multiply, 65%

Darkened text
Darken, 100%

Scotland
Hard light, 79%

California
Normal, 82%

Layering and blending

To create the final collage, I carefully sized and positioned all the elements, made most of the layers semi-opaque and applied blending modes. I used Hue-Saturation to apply a sepia-like brown tint to two of the photos and used the brush tool to paint yellow and pink strokes onto parts of the image. The final image contains twelve layers. These are shown at the top of this page in the order of layering from bottom to top and with the blending mode and opacity percentage applied to each. The version below shows what the collage looks like when all the layers are in Normal mode and 100 percent opaque. At left is the finished collage with the special blending modes and transparency in effect.

3 Using Type and Design

Typography is the craft of endowing human language with a durable visual form, and thus with an independent existence. Its heartwood is calligraphy—the dance, on a tiny stage, of the living, speaking hand—and its roots reach into living soil, though its branches may be hung each year with new machines. So long as the root lives, typography remains a source of true delight, true knowledge, true surprise.

—Robert Bringhurst,
The Elements of Typographic Style,
2nd edition (Hartley & Marks, 1996)

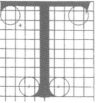

TYPOGRAPHY AND TYPESETTING—the designing and arranging of type for printing—are crafts with a rich 500-year history. The careful design of individual letters makes them easy to recognize (legible), while the spacing and arrangement of letters in lines and paragraphs makes text easy to read (readable). The design of printed pages helps the reader see and understand text and graphics in a way that is clear, uncluttered and visually pleasing.

Typesetting and page design can be done on a personal computer using a page layout program (such as PageMaker, InDesign or QuarkXPress) or in a PostScript illustration program (such as Illustrator, FreeHand or CorelDRAW). Desktop publishing software puts sophisticated typesetting and page-design tools into the hands of thousands, but without teaching the time-honored techniques of these crafts. If you're planning to work with text, it's worthwhile to learn how to use desktop publishing software and also to learn and apply the guidelines used by typographers and designers. Your work will be more finely crafted, even if you're typing just a few words for the front of a greeting card.

Typesetting Terms and Techniques

For over 400 years, from the 1440s to the late 1800s, "typesetting" was a painstaking process of setting pieces of metal type into rows for printing. This time-consuming labor was eventually relieved by the invention of typesetting machines that linked a keyboard to a metal typecasting system. Some of these, such as the Linotype, are still in use. Around the 1950s photographic typesetting methods were developed and by the 1980s typesetting became available to anyone with a personal computer and

The typefounder
Creating moveable type was once a hand craft. This woodcut showing a typefounder at work is taken from *The Book of Trades* (*Ständebuch*) published in 1568 and reprinted by Dover Publications in 1973. The German text reads: "The typefounder casts type from bismuth, tin and lead: Roman, Gothic and Greek alphabets, capital letters and punctuation marks."

page layout software. But most of the same terms and techniques of typesetting developed over the past 500 years are still in use and are applied to digital typography.

Basic type styles

Most typefaces (such as Times or Futura) consist of a family of related typefaces. (For examples of different kinds of typefaces see "Historical Typeface Styles" on page 48.) The most basic type family has four members: Roman, Italic, Bold and Bold Italic.

Roman (or Regular) is used for body text, as in the paragraphs of a novel.

Italic slants to the right and is used for *emphasis* and to *indicate titles.*

Bold is thicker than Roman and is used for **emphasis**.

***Bold Italic* is used to *set off some words* in a line that's set in Bold.**

Special type styles

In addition to the four basic styles, some typefaces include designs for extended and condensed styles (either wider than or narrower than basic Roman) as well as decorative letters, old style numbers and ligatures.

EXTENDED AND CONDENSED TYPE

Page layout programs and PostScript illustration programs have controls for making type wider or narrower. But this kind of "type mangling" distorts the carefully designed balance of thick-and-thin strokes. It's better to use specially designed condensed or expanded typefaces when these styles are needed.

Century Book

Century Book Condensed

Century Book at 85% width

OLDSTYLE NUMERALS

The arabic numerals found in most digital fonts look too large when used in paragraph text. Some fonts, such as Adobe's Garamond Expert Collection, provide oldstyle numerals that are smaller and have ascenders and descenders.

1, 2, 3, 4, 5, 6, 7, 8, 9, 0

1, 2, 3, 4, 5, 6, 7, 8, 9, 0

LIGATURES

These are pairs of letters—such as fi and fl—that look awkward next to each other and so are joined together to create a single character.

find the flag

find the flag

SWASH LETTERS

Some fonts, such as Adobe's Garamond Expert Collection, include letters with "swashes" or decorative flourishes.

*A B C D E F G H I
J K L M N O P Q R
S T U V W X Y Z*

Printing with Moveable Type

Paper and ink were both invented by the Chinese in the years from around 100 B.C. to 400 A.D. But these were used only for drawing and writing by hand until the invention of printing with type made it possible to create hundreds of sheets of writing in the time a scribe took to write one page. The key invention, moveable type, consists of small separate blocks, each with a raised letterform at the top, which can be arranged and rearranged to create any sequence of letters and words. These letterforms are spread with ink, paper is placed on top and pressed down, then peeled off to reveal the printed image. The first known pieces of type were made of clay in China around 1041 A.D. The oldest known printed page was made from metal type cast in Korea in 1397.

Metal type was invented in Europe in 1440 by the German goldsmith and jeweler Johann Gutenberg (1387–1468). His invention of printing with moveable type marked the end of the Dark Ages and the beginning of the modern age. Now thousands and thousands of people could read and learn from the classics and the new scientific literature that had previously been restricted to a few, mainly in the clergy.

Just as early motor cars looked like carriages without horses, so early books were printed with "black-letter" or "Gothic" type that imitated the look of the hand lettering done by scribes near Mainz, Germany, where Gutenberg worked. But eventually simpler and smaller letterforms based on Roman lettering were developed and standardized.

𝕿𝖞𝖕𝖊

Type

Glossary of Typography Terms

As with all crafts, typography has its own expert terminology. Learning to identify the parts of a letter will lead you to look with new eyes at the letterforms around you. The lowercase letter "g" is particularly distinctive in different typefaces.

ascender
Part of certain lowercase characters that extends above the x-height, such as the upright stroke of "b" or "d."

ascender height
The height of the ascenders in a typeface. May be higher than the cap height.

bar
The short horizontal stroke in letters such as "f," "t "and "A."

base line
The line along which the bottom of a capital letter rests.

bold or boldface
A **thicker version** of a typeface, used for emphasis.

bowl
A curved shape that creates an enclosed space in a letter.

cap height
The height of the capital letters in a typeface.

capital letters
The large letters used for beginning a sentence or a proper name. From the Latin *capitulum* (from *caput,* or "head") meaning the head or top of a pillar. Capital letters are those that "stand at the head" of a word or sentence.

caps
An abbreviation for capital letters. "All caps" means all capital letters.

character
Any element of a typeface including letters, numbers, symbols and punctuation marks. From the Latin *character*, based on Greek words meaning "to stamp, impress, engrave."

counter
The enclosed space within a character.

descender
Part of certain lowercase characters that extends below the base line, such as the tail of "p" or "g."

display type
A typeface designed to be decorative or eye-catching and meant to be used at large type sizes, such as 18 points and greater.

flush
Text that is aligned to a margin with no indentation. A paragraph can be flush left or flush right.

font
A complete set of characters designed for one typeface, including lower case, capitals, small capitals, numerals, punctuation marks, ligatures and symbols in roman, italic, boldface and so on. Often used interchangeably with typeface.

italic
A version of a typeface that is *slanted to the right*; used for emphasis and to distinguish titles and foreign words.

justified
A column of text that's adjusted so that the lines are flush with both the right and left margins.

kerning
Reducing the space between any two letters, especially in headlines, to create a more pleasing spacing.

leading
The space between the baseline of one line of text to the baseline of the line below (or above).

letter
A letter of the alphabet; from the Latin *littera*. Literary is a related word.

letterspacing
The practice of adding space between the letters of a word.

ligature
A pair of letters that are designed to fit together as one character, such as fi and fl. From the Latin verb meaning "to bind or tie."

measure
The width of a column of text, measured in picas.

margins
The areas of blank space around the edges of a printed page.

pica
A unit of type measure. One pica is equal to 12 points.

point
A unit of type measure. One point is equal to $1/72$ inch.

ragged right
A column of text set with the right-hand margin unjustified.

roman
Regular type style, as opposed to italic or boldface.

rule
A printed straight line.

serif
The small horizontal head or foot that apears at the top or bottom of the vertical stroke of a letter.

stroke
The main straight or curved line or a letter, thicker than a hairline.

superscript and subscript
Small characters that print either slightly above (super) the baseline or slightly below (sub) the baseline.

swash letters
Special decorative capital letters.

terminal
The end of a stroke, without a serif.

text
The main part or "body" of a book, usually set in a single column using a "body type" such as an oldstyle roman. Also called "body text." From the Latin *textus*, meaning the "tissue" of a literary work, or a weaving, web or texture.

type
Originally, the wooden or metal block bearing a raised character, used for printing. From the Latin *typus*, derived from a Greek word meaning "figure" or "impression," from a root meaning "to beat or strike."

typeface
A particular type design such as Bookman, Caxton, Helvetica or Times.

type style
The style—such as roman, italic, bold and so on—in a particular typeface.

x-height
The height of the lowercase characters, such as "x," that have no ascenders or descenders.

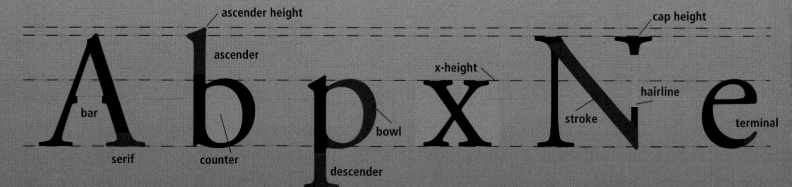

Type size

For over 400 years the size of type was designated with names—such as Great Primer—rather than numbers. In an effort to provide more uniformity, the French developed the "point" system of type measurement around 1878. A point is approximately $1/72$ of an inch and there are 12 points in a pica and 6 picas in an inch.

12-point

24-point

36-point

In the days when type was made of metal, typefaces were cast only in the most commonly used sizes. But with a computer and flexible PostScript or TrueType fonts, it's possible to change type size to any value instantly. Body text, such as that found in newspaper and magazine articles, is usually set in sizes ranging from 9 points to 14 points. Headlines are usually set in larger sizes, ranging from 16 points to 36 points and on up into the hundreds.

Since type size is measured from the lowest type feature to the highest—for example, from the lowest descender to the highest ascender—different typefaces set in the same point size can look as though they are in different sizes, especially when one is a script font with long ascenders and descenders.

14-point Palatino

14-point Charme

Type leading

Leading (rhymes with "heading") is the space, measured in points, between lines of type; specifically, between the baseline of one line to the baseline of the next. It is so called because in the early days of printing, typesetters used strips of lead to separate rows of type. Leading is important because this blank space between lines makes a block of text easier to read.

Leading should be at least 120 percent that of the type size for body text in columns that average 10 words per line. So type set in 10-point size should have 12-point leading, as in this paragraph. This provides a comfortable amount of white space above and below each line.

Page layout and word processing programs often include an "auto" or automatic leading function, with a default of 120 percent. But it may be necessary to increase the leading if the column width is wider than about twelve words. (Because the main columns in this book are fairly wide, I've set the 10.5-point text type with 16-point leading, which is 152 percent greater than the text size.)

Type set with too little leading looks cramped and the descenders of one line may collide with the ascenders of next. This paragraph is set in 12-point type with 11-point leading. "Negative leading" like this makes a text block difficult to read.

Type size and leading are often noted together with a slash separating the two numbers. For example, "10/12" means 10-point type with 12-point leading and is also said "ten on twelve."

Using Capital Letters

Setting body text in all capitals should be avoided, as it is difficult to read. But when you need to type abbreviations composed of capitals, such as CMYK, TIFF or WYSIWYG (what you see is what you get), the typesetting convention is to use small capitals or "small caps," which have a similar design, but a smaller size.

The "small caps" function provided by page layout programs approximates small caps. But true small caps are designed to have the correct thickness of stroke. So if your font does not include a set of small caps, it's better to set acronyms in all caps and reduce their type size slightly, rather than use the small caps function. It's also customary to increase the letterspacing of capitals, to enhance readability.

When acronyms such as CMYK, TIFF and WYSIWYG are typed in capital letters they look congested and too large.

Terms such as CMYK, TIFF and WYSIWYG look better in small capitals.

Historical Typeface Styles

Most digital typefaces are derived from the metal typefaces used for the past 550 years. **Serif** and **Sans Serif** are the two main classes of typefaces. (Serifs are the small heads and feet that appear at the tops and bottoms of the vertical strokes of letters.) Serif faces have serifs, while Sans ("without") Serif faces don't.

It is believed that serifs, found in early Roman carved type, may have been artifacts of the way letters were brushed onto stone before cutting. They were retained in the first cast metal type faces because they help the eye distinguish letters. Serif faces are very readable and are the most commonly used for text in books and magazines. Sans serif faces work well for headlines and subheadings. They are also used to distinguish sidebar or caption text from the main running text (as I have done by using Frutiger for the text you're reading), though in general they are less readable in smaller type sizes.

Serif typefaces
This includes four historical groups.

Venetian Oldstyle
Based on the first Roman-style typefaces that appeared in printing in Venice in the 1470s, these faces were designed to imitate scholar's handwriting.

Berkeley
Guardi

Garalde Oldstyle
Still in common use today, these were designed in the sixteenth and seventeenth centuries and have more contrast between thick and thin lines than the Venetian styles

Caxton
Goudy

Transitional
Designed in the eighteenth century, these share features of both Oldstyle and Modern serif faces.

Janson
Times

Didone or Modern
Improvements in printing made it possible to design and use typefaces with very thin serifs.

Bodoni
Fenice

Slab serif
These typefaces, also called square serif, were developed in the early nineteenth century for advertising and have heavy, block serifs to catch attention.

Clarendon
Glypha

Sans serif typefaces
Distinctly modern typefaces with no serifs; popular in the 1920s, inspired by the "less is more" Bauhaus design philosophy. There are four main types of sans serif typefaces.

Grotesque sans serif
These were called "grotesque" by the English who considered them ugly.

Franklin Gothic
Tempo Heavy Condensed

Neo-grotesque sans serif
These more recent Swiss-style sans serifs are more graceful.

Frutiger
Helvetica

Geometric sans serif
These Bauhaus-influenced faces use circles and other geometric shapes.

Bauhaus
Futura

Humanist sans serif
More organic looking shapes with some thick-and-thin variation.

Gill Sans
Optima

Script typefaces
first designed in the 1600s, script typefaces imitate handwriting, both cursive (connected letters) and printed (separate letters).

Formal script typefaces

Brush Script
Kaufmann
Snell Roundhand

Casual script typefaces

Dom Casual
Freestyle Script
Mistral

Glyphic typefaces
Based on carved rather than written letter forms. Many of these typefaces have capital letters only, following the Roman style.

LITHOS
RUSTICANA
TRAJAN

Blackletter typefaces
Also called Old English or Gothic, this ornate type is based on early German moveable type designs that imitated manuscript writing done with a broad, flat-tipped pen.

Duc De Berry
Fette Fraktur
Notre Dame

Display typefaces
These typefaces may be old or new, serif or sans serif, but all are designed to look best at large sizes for use as headlines and titles. These typefaces are difficult to read when set in small sizes for blocks of type.

Arnold Böcklin
Cooper Black
ROSEWOOD
STENCIL

Symbol typefaces
These include Carta, used for cartography (map making), Symbol, with marks for science and mathematics, and Zapf Dingbats, a collection of ornaments. (Just a few characters from each font are shown.)

CARTA

SYMBOL

θ ω ε ρ ψ υ ο φ γ δ
ξ ϖ β μ ™ [Θ Ε Τ
Υ Ο { Δ Γ ϑ Λ ®

ZAPF DINGBATS

Type spacing

Spacing is the amount of lateral space between letters and words (as opposed to *leading*, the vertical spacing between lines.) Most typewriters use *fixed-width spacing*, with each letter taking up the same amount of horizontal space. But professional typesetting uses proportional spacing, with each letter taking up only as much space as it needs. Most digital fonts are proportionally spaced, producing type that looks better and allows more characters per line.

```
Courier is a fixed-
width typeface.
```

Souvenir is a proportional typeface.

LETTERSPACING

Proportional type is designed with *letterspacing* (spaces between the characters) that optimizes readability. But sometimes the default letterspacing should be increased or decreased. For example, type set in all capitals often looks crowded and should have its letterspacing increased.

LETTERS SET IN ALL CAPS

LOOK BETTER WITH MORE LETTERSPACING

Sometimes wide letterspacing is used to create a special effect and make a line of type look like a border element.

UNDERSTANDING

U N D E R S T A N D I N G

KERNING

Letterspacing is designed to optimize readability at body text sizes. But when the letters appear in larger sizes—in headlines, for example—the space between them can look too great. *Kerning* means decreasing the space between individual pairs of letters at larger point sizes. In the example below I kerned the space between the "P" and the "E" and between the "A" and the "C."

PEACE

PEACE

Aligning columns of text

Columns of body text can be aligned in four ways: flush left, flush right, centered or justified. These are often called "paragraph styles" in page layout programs. Flush left is a common and reader-friendly style, with a more casual feeling than justified text. Flush right is harder to read but is used sometimes for graphic effect. Centered columns of type are used mainly for invitations and announcement and sometimes for poetry. Justified columns are commonly used in books as well as in newspapers and magazines.

When type is centered or set flush to only one margin, the spacing between the words remains constant. However, when type is justified the space between the words must be varied for each line, according to how many words there are in the line. This makes a justified column more of a challenge to the typesetter, for it can sometimes

Typing on a Computer

Those of us born before 1965 probably first learned to set type on a typewriter. But to paraphrase computer writer Robin Williams, *the computer is not a typewriter*. Different rules apply and to get the best results with a computer it's best to follow the rules.

1. Type *only one space*, not two, after periods, commas and all other punctuation marks.

2. Use curved typographers quotes (such as these: " ") and curved apostrophes rather than the straight line marks used to designate feet and inches. Some programs make it possible to turn on these curly marks (called "smart quotes") so that they're automatically produced when you hit the quote/apostrophe key. (Note that some typefaces, such as the Frutiger used for this sidebar text, include stylized quotes and apostrophes that are not very curly.)

3. Never use underlined type. To add *emphasis*, use italics. Also use italics to indicate a title, such as *War and Peace*.

4. TYPE THAT IS SET IN ALL CAPITAL LETTERS IS DIFFICULT TO READ. For headlines use a larger type size, rather than all caps. For emphasis, use **boldface** (sparingly) or *italics*.

5. Use hyphens and dashes appropriately:
• An *em dash* (—) is a dash that's about the width of a letter "M." Use it to set off a parenthetical thought, indicate a break or to set off the beginning of a line. On a Mac, type Option-Shift-Hyphen to get an em dash. In Windows type Alt 0151 on the keypad.
• An *en dash* (–), about the width of a letter "N," is used to separate numbers in dates and times of day (as in 1949–2001). On a Mac, type Option-Hyphen to get an en dash. In Windows type Alt 0150 on the keypad.
• A *hyphen* (-) is used to hyphenate words or to separate numbers in a phone number or zip code.

6. Use your spell checker, but be aware that it won't alert you to words that are wrongly used, but correctly spelled, such as "Let's go to a party at *there* house."

The graphic signs called letters are so completely blended with the stream of written thought that their presence therein is as unperceived as the ticking of a clock in the measurement of time. Only by an effort of attention does the layman discover that they exist at all. It comes to him as a surprise that these signs should be a matter of concern to any one of the crafts of men.

But to be concerned with the shapes of letters is to work in an ancient and fundamental material. The qualities of letterforms at their best are the qualities of a classic time: order, simplicity, grace. To try to learn and repeat their excellence is to put oneself under training in a simple and severe school of design.

—William Addison Dwiggens, type designer

result in artificially tight lines (too little word spacing) or loose lines (too much word spacing). Traditionally, this problem has been solved using careful hyphenation of words and this method is also used with computer type.

The text used in the column style examples below is from *The Elements of Typographic Style* (Hartley & Marks, 1996), by Robert Bringhurst, a typographer who is also a poet. As you can see, justified type takes up the least space.

For all the beauty of pure geometry, a perfectly square block of type on a perfectly square page with even margins all around is a form unlikely to encourage reading. Reading, like walking, involves navigation—and the square block of type on a square block of paper is short of basic landmarks and clues. To give the reader a sense of direction, and the page a sense of liveliness and poise, it is necessary to break this inexorable sameness and find a new balance of another kind. Some space must be narrow so that other space may be wide, and some space emptied so that other space may be filled.
Flush left, Times Roman, 9/11

For all the beauty of pure geometry, a perfectly square block of type on a perfectly square page with even margins all around is a form unlikely to encourage reading. Reading, like walking, involves navigation—and the square block of type on a square block of paper is short of basic landmarks and clues. To give the reader a sense of direction, and the page a sense of liveliness and poise, it is necessary to break this inexorable sameness and find a new balance of another kind. Some space must be narrow so that other space may be wide, and some space emptied so that other space may be filled.
Centered, Times Roman, 9/11

For all the beauty of pure geometry, a perfectly square block of type on a perfectly square page with even margins all around is a form unlikely to encourage reading. Reading, like walking, involves navigation—and the square block of type on a square block of paper is short of basic landmarks and clues. To give the reader a sense of direction, and the page a sense of liveliness and poise, it is necessary to break this inexorable sameness and find a new balance of another kind. Some space must be narrow so that other space may be wide, and some space emptied so that other space may be filled.
Flush right, Times Roman, 9/11

For all the beauty of pure geometry, a perfectly square block of type on a perfectly square page with even margins all around is a form unlikely to encourage reading. Reading, like walking, involves navigation—and the square block of type on a square block of paper is short of basic landmarks and clues. To give the reader a sense of direction, and the page a sense of liveliness and poise, it is necessary to break this inexorable sameness and find a new balance of another kind. Some space must be narrow so that other space may be wide, and some space emptied so that other space may be filled.
Justified, Times Roman, 9/11

COLUMN WIDTH

Columns that are too wide make it hard for our eyes to scan from the end of one line back to the start of the one below. One rule of thumb is that a line should have a maximum of 55 to 60 characters or about 9 or 10 words. If your column is wider (for example, when typing a school paper in one wide column on letter-sized paper) the amount of leading should be increased. That's one reason why many teachers insist that term papers be "double-spaced," meaning that the leading size is doubled. (For examples see the section on "type leading" on page 47.)

Experimenting with Type

There are many ways to go beyond the usual typefaces used in digital design. You might want to use your own handwriting, or create "found type" by scanning household objects that resemble letterforms. You can also create "distressed" type or use one of the grunge fonts that's grown out of the punk movement.

Adding handwritten type

Scanning a sample of your own handwriting is one way to provide contrast for the regularity of computer-generated type.

Hand lettering can be a welcome visual relief.

Cropping type

Try obscuring the top or bottom edge of a large headline, just enough to create a graphic effect, but not enough to make the text unreadable.

TYPE CAN BE LEGIBLE,
THOUGH PARTLY HIDDEN

Creating distressed type

Try scanning and enlarging type created on an old typewriter, or else enlarge computer or typewriter type on an office copier until it starts to break up and become irregular. Then scan the photocopy.

Found type

Letterforms abound in nature and in the contents of our kitchen drawers. Objects can be scanned and silhouetted to create interesting and decorative initial capitals.

Using a Grunge Typeface

Most of the typefaces provided by digital type companies are based on fonts created by traditional type foundries over the past 400 years. But since the personal computer has made it possible for "outsiders" to create digital fonts, there's been an explosion of new typefaces, some of which are controversial. One of my favorites of the new digital type design companies is House Industries, based in Wilmington, Delaware, which provides a collection of Bad Neighborhood Fonts that includes the infamous, but widely used font Crackhouse. (Some of the fonts below are used in the accordion book shown on page 96). Dover Publications also publishes an inexpensive collective of "grunge" typefaces on CD-ROM.

Sometimes a typeface like Crackhouse is just the right font for the message. Or you might want to use Dirtyhouse, or Openhouse or Poorhouse.

To live a creative life, we must lose our fear of being wrong.
—Joseph Chilton Pearce

The Basics of Graphic Design

Look at the printed material around you—ads, books, magazines, packaging, brochures, posters. What appeals to you and what doesn't? Which designs catch your eye and which leave you cold? Breaking these designs down into their components makes it possible to find out what makes them work or not work.

Elements of design

All graphic designs are made up of basic elements or building blocks that can be combined in various ways.

LINE

Linear elements, straight and curved, have qualities such as thickness, spacing, direction, repetition and texture. Lines create shapes and also divide space into shapes.

SHAPE

Lines, letterforms, text blocks, photos and so on, have shape and so do the spaces between these elements.

TEXTURE

Surface interest and structure can be created by a design as a whole, as well as by its individual elements, such as background designs or blocks of type.

SPACE

Space is not created directly, but results from the placement of elements. It includes the "negative space" between and around graphic elements.

VALUE

Value or tone is created by the lightness or darkness of type or design elements.

COLOR

The hue (such as yellow, blue-green or violet) of text or design elements is a source of emotional power.

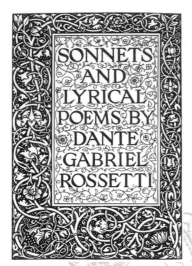

Surface patterns
The complex and curving ornaments that adorn this 1894 title page by William Morris create a rich sense of texture. The page is from *200 Decorative Title Pages* by Alexander Nesbitt (Dover, 1964).

Shades and tones
In this detail from an ancient Greek border, solid black and white are combined with golds of differing value. The value differences can be seen clearly when the image is converted to grayscale. The art is from *The Grammar of Ornament* by Owen Jones (Dover, 1987).

Sinewy line
In nature, a sense of line is created by the edges of objects. This is portrayed in art in a stylized way by drawing lines with pen and ink, as in the curving outline of a starfish (see background illustration) from *Art Forms in Nature* by Ernst Haeckel (Dover, 1974).

Brilliant color
Strong colors attract the eye, as in this fruit crate label. The design also has strong line quality (see the title type and the cat's outline) as well as effective contrast between light and dark areas and a balanced composition that leaves the viewer's eye as stable and rested as the cat. The label is from *Full Color Fruit Crate Labels: CD-ROM and Book* (Dover, 2000).

Principles of design

Design principles are based on fundamental human ways of perceiving and organizing visual information. If you're having trouble figuring how best to combine text and graphics, use the basic design principles to help you create "solutions" to graphic design problems.

UNITY

Graphic elements are unified when they look as though they belong together. Unity can be produced by combining similar elements or by arranging dissimilar elements in an orderly way. *Proximity* achieves unity by placing elements that are related near each other. *Repetition* creates unity by duplicating design elements in rows, grids or radial designs.

VARIETY

Unity is complemented by variety, which can be achieved by creating variations on a theme and also through the use of contrast. *Contrast* can be created by opposing the two polarities found in any visual quality, including value (light/dark), weight (thick/thin), form (linear/curved), quantity (many/few), texture (dense/open) and scale (large/small).

BALANCE

Balance creates a sense of stability and equal weight among different parts of a design, as though all were distributed along the horizontal bar of a teeter-totter. Balance can be symmetrical or asymmetrical and horizontal, vertical or radial.

RHYTHM

A sense of visual rhythm occurs when objects are repeated, distributed or varied in ways that create the feeling of a pulse that beats, flows, swirls or builds to a climax.

EMPHASIS

Emphasis is created when elements and their arrangement lead the eye toward the most important part of a design.

PROPORTION AND SCALE

Proportion refers to the relationship between elements of different sizes within a whole (for example, the size of the nose in relation to the eyes and mouth), while scale refers to size in relation to units of measure such as points or inches.

Variety and rhythm
Three similar fish are varied in color and arranged in a flowing rhythmical composition in this contemporary paper kite design by Fort Bragg, California artist Christine Schomer.

Game of balance
The King of Hearts from an antique Swiss card deck is symmetrically balanced across the horizontal axis, with a rhythmic, almost circular intertwining of the King's arms and hands at the center. The card design also displays a strong use of shape, repetition and a careful arrangement of positive and negative space.

Ideal proportion
In 1528 the master German artist Albrecht Dürer superimposed grid lines over two views of a nude to illustrate his theories on the ideal proportions of the female body.

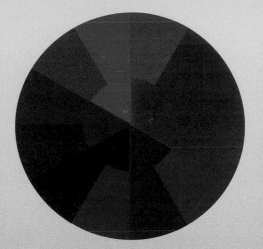

Working with Color

The traditional color wheel can be a great help in choosing colors that will look harmonious together. Below are five traditional color schemes. (For information on how computers handle color see "Understanding Color Models" on pages 22–23.)

Complements
Any two colors that are opposite each other on a color wheel.

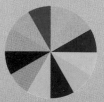

Double complements
Any pair of complementary colors.

Creating a color wheel

The three primary color pigments—red, blue and yellow—cannot be mixed from any other colors. The primaries can be mixed with each other to create the secondary colors—purple, green and orange. The primaries and secondaries can be mixed with each other to create six more intermediate colors, making the 12 colors of a traditional color wheel. You might like to use your image-editing or drawing program to create a 12-color wheel and use it as a palette for some of your artwork. Tints can be created by reducing color strength to around 50 percent, while shades can be created by adding 15 percent black.

Near complements
A color plus the two colors that are on either side of its complement.

Triadic complements
A group of three colors that are equidistant from each other around a color wheel.

Multiple complements or analogous colors
A group of colors that are adjacent to each other on a color wheel.

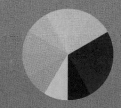

FIND IT IN *START WITH A SCAN*
For more examples of color wheels and combinations see pages 32–33 of *Start with a Scan*, (Peachpit Press, 2000).

A Simple Four-Step Design Process

If you apply certain simple design guidelines, your page designs—business cards, flyers, newsletters and so on—will be bolder, more attractive, better organized and have a more finished, professional look.

Step 1: Type and organize

ASSEMBLE TEXT AND GRAPHICS

Before you start designing, make sure you know what you want to say. Write out all the text that will be used. If your design announces an event be sure to include the journalist's "five W's": *who, what, where, when* and *why.* Gather any photos or other graphics you want to include and scan and edit them.

OPEN A LAYOUT FILE

Open a new file in your chosen page size in an appropriate program, either a word processing program (such as WordPerfect or Word), or page layout program (such as PageMaker or QuarkXPress) or PostScript illustration program (such as Illustrator or FreeHand). To create the business card shown below, I used PageMaker.

First acquire an infallible technique and then open yourself to inspiration.
—Japanese saying

Even when laws have been written down, they ought not always to remain unaltered.
—Aristotle (384–322 B.C.)

Designing a Business Card

Far From Home
A violin and button accordion duo
Based in Mendocino, California

Playing the music of immigrants to California from New England, Britain, France, Italy, Spain, Portugal and Mexico

Available for weddings, parties, special events
Call 707/937-4558 or 964-7114

1 Type text and organize into logical groups
All the type is set in Times Roman, 10/12

Far From Home

A violin and button accordion duo
Based in Mendocino, California

Playing the music of immigrants to California from New England, Britain, France, Italy, Spain, Portugal and Mexico

Available for weddings, parties, special events
Call 707/937-4558 or 964-7114

2 Create emphasis
The band name is most important so it's set in 24-point type.

Far From Home
A violin and button accordion duo
Based in Mendocino, California

Playing the music of immigrants to California from New England, Britain, France, Italy, Spain, Portugal and Mexico

Weddings, parties, special events
707/937-4558 or 964-7114

3 Position elements to organize contents
The band name, personnel and location are kept at the left while the rest of the information is moved to the right. Type size and letterspacing are adjusted to create aligned text blocks. The card is now functional and easy to read, but not very distinctive. Let's take it one step further.

FAR FROM HOME
A Violin and Button Accordion Duo
• MENDOCINO • CALIFORNIA •

Playing the music of immigrants to California from New England, Britain, France, Italy, Spain, Portugal and Mexico

WEDDINGS·PARTIES·SPECIAL EVENTS
707-937-4558 or 964-7114

4 Create interest with contrast and repetition
Reversing "Far from Home" over solid black creates contrast and using the same treatment for the phone numbers creates repetition. All caps and increased letterspacing on some text varies the Times Roman and one text block is set in contrasting Helvetica Condensed.

Far
from
Home

**A Violin and
Button Accordion Duo**

MENDOCINO, CALIFORNIA

*Playing the music of immigrants to
California from New England,
Britain, France, Italy, Spain,
Portugal and Mexico*

**WEDDINGS • PARTIES
SPECIAL EVENTS**

707/937-4558 or 964-3114

Fine tuning the design
A second design takes the business card on the
previous page in a different direction. Making
the card format vertical creates a sense of
surprise, while changing the text to an old style
Italian typeface, Guardia, emphasizes the fact
that the band plays the music of our ancestors.
A warm beige paper and traditional rust red
reinforce the antique look, as does the use of a
nineteenth century printer's ornament, taken
from Adobe's Woodtype Ornaments 2 typeface.
Use of centered alignment completes the
traditional look.

CHOOSE A PAGE SIZE

Think about how the piece will be
printed (on your own printer at home?)
and what sizes of paper can be used. If
your piece will be mailed, choose a
paper size that fits into standard size
envelopes. If your piece will be posted
on a bulletin board, make sure it's large
enough to be seen. If your piece will be
handed out at an event, make it a
convenient size for people to put into a
purse or pocket. If your final page size
will be less than a standard-size sheet,
save time and money by making it a
multiple of this size: either a half, third
or quarter.

TYPE ALL THE TEXT

Don't worry about organizing at this
point, just get all the text typed in and
do a final edit to make sure it's accurate,
clearly written and correctly spelled.
Double check your dates and facts, if
you have any.

ORGANIZE TEXT INTO GROUPS

One simple way to organize text is to
group it according to whether it describes the who, what, where, when or
why of your message. Probably the
"what" will be your main emphasis and
will end up at or near the top of the
page (though not always).

Step 2: Create emphasis

Make your main message stand out by
setting it apart visually from other text.
Do this by making it a larger size, a
heavier weight, or a brighter color; by
adding a bullet or ornament; or by
adding a photo or picture.

Step 3: Align and position elements

Align the elements within each text
group so that they look unified and
work together as a group. Alignment
can either be flush left, flush right or
centered. Position the groups so that
they look coherent on the page. Use an
underlying grid to help with alignment
and positioning. (Page layout and illustration programs provide column guides
and grids that can be used for alignment.) Don't place elements randomly
on the page, but make sure they are all
positioned in some logical way, either
aligned with each other or to a grid.

Step 4: Create interest

CREATE CONTRAST

Create emphasis and visual excitement
by exaggerating the differences between different parts of your design.
For example, the main title can be set in
type that's *much larger* than all the
other text or could be colored white
and placed on a black background.
Contrast can also be created by using
different typefaces (such as an old style
serif face that contrasts with a modern
sans serif), different weights (light versus bold), and different colors or shades
of gray.

USE REPETITION

To create a sense of rhythm on your
page, chose some element of the design and repeat it. For example, a small
dingbat used at 100 percent black at the
end of a line of type could also be
blown up to fill almost the entire page
and used as a background element at 10
percent black.

The Gestalt of Design

Gestalt is a German word that we translate roughly as *wholeness*, as in the sense of a whole being greater or *different* than the sum of its parts. For example, a melody is different than a group of single notes—it has a *gestalt* that goes beyond its component parts. Gestalt principles, developed by German and Austrian psychologists around 1912, are based on studies of human perception and can be applied to help us develop graphic designs that are in sympathy with human perceptual preferences.

1. Figure/Ground
The contrast between objects and backgrounds makes it possible for us to see them.

2. Equilibrium
Physical processes tend toward stable states and people prefer to see stable, resting shapes.

3. Isomorphic correspondence
Visual forms and symbols that are similar to real events evoke similar emotional responses.

4. Continuation
The eye tends to travel along and then beyond lines or curves in the visual field.

5. Closure
Closed shapes are perceived as more stable than open shapes. Incomplete shapes generate visual interest as our brains try to close them by mentally filling the gaps.

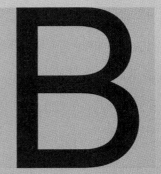

6. Proximity
The eye is drawn to visual elements that are near each other, forming groups.

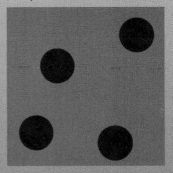
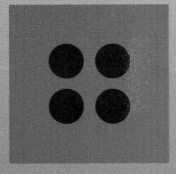

7. Similarity
Similar objects are perceived as a group and dissimilar objects stand out from the group.

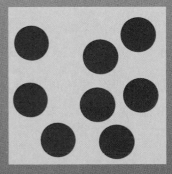

Using a Grid

Grids are networks of vertical or horizontal guidelines—something like graph paper—that help organize graphic elements. Even though the grid itself is not usually visible, the visual organization it provides is sensed and appreciated by the viewer. In a page layout or illustration program you can set up guidelines and also single- or multi-column grids. These guidelines will be visible on screen to help you in positioning and sizing graphics and blocks of text, but will not appear when the page is printed.

Violate the grid
Establishing a grid and placing most elements in alignment with it makes it possible to create drama by letting some elements pop in or out. For example, you can break into a rectangular text block by a positioning a graphic partly into the column and wrapping the text around it.

Establish rules, then break them

It's important to escape from the confines of a grid from time to time, for too much regularity is dull and leads to visual boredom. Just as infants can fearlessly explore so long as mother is nearby, so viewers enjoy seeing pictures and words break out of the safety of a rectangular grid system, so long as they still feel a sense of the underlying structure. There are various ways to "break out of the box."

Vary the shapes of graphics. Rather than rectangular photos and graphics, use full or partial silhouettes, such as the engraving of a pointing girl at left.

Use bleeds. Let graphic elements "bleed" off the page by extending them beyond the page margins, as with the green sidebar background on the opposite page.

Experiment with sizes and placement of elements. In a three-column grid, for example, pictures can be one, two, or three columns wide.

Varying the shapes of text blocks
For over 500 years, typesetters have experimented with creating text blocks that have shapes other than square. The book design below features a single column design with an outside margin containing a running head. On the verso page (left side), the typesetter has arranged the text so that it tapers into a triangle, finished off by a triangular type ornament, thus marking the end of a section. On the recto page (right side) the text column beginning the next section is penetrated at the top left by a large decorative capital. This two-page spread was scanned from a small book entitled *Little Journeys to the Homes of Great Musicians: Sebastian Bach*, part of a series written by Elbert Hubbard and printed by him on a letterpress in 1901 at The Roycrofters, a collective in East Aurora, New York that specialized in limited edition hand-printed and sewn books. The Roycrofters were part of the "Arts and Crafts" movement of artisans who reacted to the mechanization of modern life by returning to the hand-crafting techniques and values of earlier centuries.

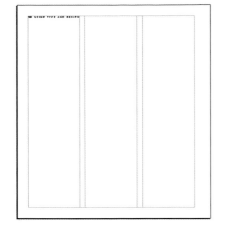

Jump out of the grid

The page design of *The Arts and Crafts Computer* is based on a three-column grid (above). Most of the captions are one column wide while most of the main text is in two-column wide blocks. Most illustrations are either one, two or three columns wide. This provides a pleasing and flexible framework, but if I kept to it slavishly the pages would look static. Compare a grid-governed layout (above right) with the actual page 58.

Free the trapped white space

One simple but powerful way to improve any design is to look for areas of "trapped white space"— blank areas surrounded on all sides by text or graphics—and rearrange elements so that the trapped space has at least one avenue of escape to the margins of the page. The layout at right, with its small island of trapped white space, makes me feel claustrophobic, while the actual layout of page 58 feels open, dynamic and relaxed.

Exaggerate the grid

One way to organize a lot of disparate elements is to place them very strictly into an orderly grid system such as a checkerboard design. This Christmas card design made by my daughter Florence Ashford uses a 3 by 6 block grid to organize nine differently shaped holiday graphics and nine Victorian-style decorative letters. All the elements were scanned from Dover clip-art books, edited in Photoshop and placed in a PageMaker layout.

Is it so important in this age of nuclear threat, AIDS, terrorism and polyester shirts that magazine covers, building entrances, corporate logos, lipstick ads or abstract collages be beautiful?

Was it important that Haydn played beautifully at Prince Esterházy's musical soirées for 80 people? That Dürer signed his etchings in much more elegant lettering than is available from all of today's computer typesetting marvels? That Stradivari treated the wood of the violins he built for a handful of clients in Cremona in a way that hasn't been duplicated in four centuries?

Yes. The answer is yes, it is important. It is the small monuments, the details that are the milestones of civilization; they accumulate to make history. Sometimes I feel that we are near the entrance to a tunnel leading into a long night, and we must leave marks before the darkness.

—Henry Wolf, *Visual Thinking: Methods for Making Images Memorable* (American Showcase, 1988)

Creative Design Techniques

An adequate design—for a parking ticket or a telephone bill, for example—organizes and presents information clearly. A great design goes one step further, using elegance, charm, drama or wit to engage the viewer and present information in a way that's memorable. There are various ways to transform a design from *good enough* to special. Two especially effective devices are exaggeration and surprise.

Exaggerate design principles

"Don't be a wimp!" says designer and author Robin Williams. Exaggerate your use of the basic design elements and principles (see pages 52–53). Make a large letter *very* large. Make a dark area *very* dark. Get into the habit of looking at your designs with a designer's eye to find ways to make them more dynamic by exaggerating elements of line, shape, texture, space, orientation or value, or principles of balance, unity, proximity, repetition or contrast.

Surprise the viewer

EXPERIMENT WITH CROPPING

Use unusual proportions. Photographs and other rectangular artwork need not always have the proportions of a postcard. Try cropping a photo to create a tall, thin version, or a wide, thin version that creates a horizontal border.

Focus by cropping. Crop full format photographs down to their dramatic details in order to focus on essentials. For example, a full portrait could be cropped down to zero in on just the eyes, nose and mouth at the center of the face.

Fade away. Instead of using four hard edges, experiment with filters in Photoshop to make one edge of a photograph fade gradually to white.

USE UNEXPECTED COMBINATIONS

The Surrealist painter Rene Magritte was a master of surprise, painting a locomotive emerging from a fireplace and a room wallpapered with the sky. His combinations were sometimes the result of dreams and were part of his exploration of the nature of visual reality. What unusual combinations of text or image can you imagine?

RE-PURPOSE FAMILIAR DESIGN STYLES

One designer used familiar red-and-white-striped popcorn bags as envelopes for party invitations. The bags immediately stimulate anticipation of food and fun.

Unusual proportions

My photo of the flower fields in Carlsbad, California is good enough in its standard 35mm film format. But it becomes more interesting when I crop it to exaggerate its proportions. The tall version would make an attractive bookmark, while the wide version could become a border for a sheet of family stationery. To soften the boxy shape of the photo, I used Photoshop to fade it to white at the bottom. To do this I placed a black to white gradient in an alpha channel at the bottom of the image, loaded the channel and then deleted the graduated selection.

Exaggerate differences

Customers know which cab driver to request when they get this business card designed by my son Rufus Ashford. The oversized numeral catches the eye and provides strong visual contrast with the other elements of the design.

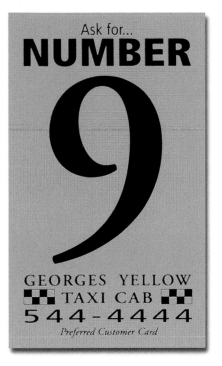

Surprise, surprise

An anonymous artist has been stamping dollar bills to raise awareness about the legal status of hemp (see "The Politics of Paper" on page 69. One of them found its way into my wallet. This piece of social activism is an example of the power of surprise, unexpected combinations and the re-purposing of a familiar design. Altering currency designs to make a point has a long history, but be aware that scanning, photographing and reproducing paper currency at actual size is illegal. (For more uses of currency in design see "Decorating Everyday Objects" on page 114.)

Encouraging Creativity

Here are a few tips to use when you want to jump start a creative idea or short circuit a creative block.

Keep a swipes pile

Set aside a large box or folder for saving inspirational items that come your way; mailers, magazines, photos, and so on.

Enhance your work place

Keep a bouquet of fresh flowers on your desk. Listen to nice music.

Take a break

Sketch or doodle

Clean your work space

Take a walk

Take in the visual variety on your street or walk in a park or on a nature trail.

Visit a museum

Look at the exhibits, jot down ideas, check out the gift shop.

Go shopping

Not necessarily to buy anything but to get inspiration. Visit junk stores, arts supply stores, shops carrying ethnic art and so on. Notice graphic elements such as the color and shape of objects, the design of packaging and the spacial arrangement and decoration of the store.

Suspend judgement

Try to keep your inner critic out of the way. Notice any negative inner judgements that occur. See what happens if you say "thank you" to your vigilant inner judge and then let those judgments go.

Don't be an idiot

The French surrealist André Breton wrote, "The man who cannot visualize a horse galloping on a tomato is an idiot." That maxim applies to women as well, I suppose. I combined a tomato scanned from an old seed catalog and a galloping horse and rider scanned from *Handbook of Early Advertising Art* (Dover, 1956). Color was added to the black and white scans using the techniques described in "Adding a Color Layer" on page 35.

4 Gathering Art Supplies

TROLLING THROUGH AN ART SUPPLY STORE is a pleasure. Just the sight of beautifully colored paints and pencils is exciting—I'd like to buy one of everything! But I've learned that art materials do not make an artist and that it's better to *create* than to *buy*. So instead of a shopping trip, make a drawing right now with whatever pencils, pens and paper are around. Try working with these tools for a few weeks, then add a few inexpensive items from the drug store—a box of children's watercolors, some colored pencils, some crayons. See what you can do with these for a few months, drawing and painting the people and things around you. When the time is right, make your trip to the art supply store. You'll know what you want—and you'll already be a practicing artist.

Drawing and Painting

Drawing and painting are the most fundamental ways to express ourselves in visual art. There are many types of paints and drawing materials, each with its own characteristics and special techniques. To learn more about basic art materials, visit your local museum, take a class or read a book on technique.

Self-portrait with Art Materials
Acrylic on canvas, Janet Isaacs Ashford, 1990.

Paints

Paint consists of a colored pigment combined with a binder. The finely powdered pigment provides the color, while the binder provides a way of mixing the pigment and applying it to a surface. Different binders produce different types of art media, each with their own uses and techniques.

WATER SOLUBLE PAINTS

Water-based paints are the easiest and safest to use.

Watercolor paints are made of powdered pigments mixed with gum arabic. (Gum arabic is a hardened sap from acacia trees.) Watercolors come in dried cakes (to be mixed with water) or in liquid form in tubes and bottles. They are semitransparent and can be diluted with water to produce a wide range of strengths from intense, rich colors to pale tints. They're usually applied to textured papers, on which they act something like a stain. Watercolorists work from light to dark and often let the whiteness of the paper show through. These paints range in quality from the children's sets sold in drug stores (see "Keeping It Simple" on the next page) to professional materials.

Tempera paint, sometimes called "egg tempera," is traditionally made by mixing egg yolk emulsion with powdered pigments. It's one of the earliest Western fine arts paints, used for painting frescoes and alter pieces in medieval Europe. It was largely replaced by oil paint in the 1500s, but egg tempera is still handmade and used by enthusiasts. These days tempera is also made with synthetic materials and used in schools. It is an opaque paint, something like poster paint.

Gouache (also called designer's color or body color) is similar to watercolor, but the colored pigments are mixed with white pigment and extender to make them opaque. Available in both tubes and cakes, it's especially good for producing areas of solid, rich color and can be used on both paper and board. It's often sold in paintbox sets, which are convenient to use.

Acrylic. First used by fine artists in the 1940s, acrylic paint is made by mixing pigments with synthetic resin made from acrylic acid. It's opaque, can be used on many surfaces, dries quickly and has a matte finish when dry (though it can be mixed with a gloss medium to give the paint a shine). Acrylic paint can be brushed on thickly, but because it is fast-drying it can't be manipulated as oil paint can be. It can be thinned with water to use as a wash and can be used as an underpainting layer for oil paint. Acrylic paint can also be floated on gel to create patterns for paper marbling.

OIL PAINTS

Oil paints are made of pigments mixed with oil—traditionally linseed oil—which produces a thick, creamy paint that dries slowly, providing time for blending of color areas. As it dries, it develops a hard film that protects the brightness of the colors. Oil paints are thinned with turpentine or mineral spirits which give off hazardous fumes and should be used where ventilation is good.

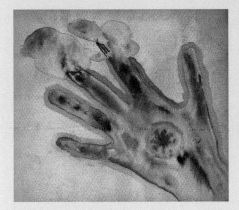

Hand in the Clouds
Watercolor on watercolor paper,
Janet Isaacs Ashford, 1970.

Keeping It Simple

Don't be discouraged if you can't afford the best quality art materials. Sometimes working with simple materials is best, as Natalie Goldberg discovered. She describes her first experience with painting in her book *Living Color: A Writer Paints Her World* (Bantam Books, 1997).

"Twenty years ago, I was teaching part-time at an alternative elementary school in Taos. I borrowed one of those inexpensive boxes of kids' watercolors—an oblong case that snapped open, with six cakes of primary color and a ridiculous paintbrush with the bristles so awry they looked like cat's whiskers. I got a cheap sketch pad at the drugstore and I began to paint. In those years, because I had little money… it never occurred to me to buy a better brush or paints. I worked for two years with only the six basic colors….

"This turned out to be a great advantage …I noticed that the blue of my paints wasn't blue enough to get the intensity of that New Mexico sky. I painted the sky red instead…. I was delighted one day to paint an adobe house blue….Objects began to dance unhinged from their proper pigment. That man is green, those sheep are maroon, that horse is scarlet, I suddenly wanted to shout with a new-found freedom…"

Forest by the Ocean
Gouache on watercolor paper, Janet Isaacs Ashford, 1994.

Brushes

Good brushes are expensive, so be sure to clean and store them carefully.

BRUSHES FOR WATERCOLORS

Watercolor brushes can also be used for gouache, acrylic and tempera. They include round, flat and fan-shaped styles made of sable fur, camel hair and synthetic fibers.

BRUSHES FOR OIL-BASED PAINTS

Brushes for oil paints are made of heavier bristles and come in round, flat and fan shapes in many sizes. They can also be used with acrylic paints.

Drawing media

PENCILS

Pencils consist of a column of black or colored drawing material encased in a wooden stylus. Pencils are often called "lead pencils," but they don't actually contain lead, which is a hazardous material. These familiar instruments feel good in the hand, are easy to control and come in a variety of media.

Graphite drawing pencils. Developed in the late 1700s, these pencils are made of a compressed mixture of graphite (a form of carbon) and clay. The more clay in the mixture, the softer will be the mark produced by the pencil. Used for sketching, graphic pencils range from very hard (8H) to very soft (8B).

Colored pencils. Also used for sketching and for adding color to drawings, colored pencils were developed in the late 1800s and are made of pigment, clay, lubricant and binder. Colored-pencil strokes can be overlaid onto paint, crayon or pastel work to create textural effects. Some brands are waterproof.

Watercolor pencils. These pencils mark with dry paint that blends together when brushed with water.

Snow White and Rose Red
Colored pencil and India ink on Bristol board, Janet Isaacs Ashford, 1990.

Shoes
Pencil sketch on newsprint (left), oil on canvas (right), Janet Isaacs Ashford, 1975.

Hazards of Art Materials

Art materials are beautiful and full of creative potential, but it's important to be aware that some of these wonderful substances contain poisonous or toxic materials.

The hazards of color

Some pigments are hazardous to our health, especially those made from metals. Because of lobbying at the state and federal levels by Ralph Nader's Public Interest Research Group, hazardous paints are now required to carry special warning labels (according to the Federal Hazardous Substances Act and the Labeling of Hazardous Art Materials Act of 1988) and toxic materials are banned from public schools. Artists using hazardous materials should wear gloves and dust masks approved by the National Institute of Occupational Safety and Health. The more often hazardous substances are used, the more health damage is done (cumulative exposure). So it's best to substitute safer materials whenever possible.

Where do color pigments come from?

Pigments are made from a variety of plant and animal materials, earth substances and metals.

- **Natural inorganic pigments** are made from earth and are the oldest known pigments: yellow ocher, slate grey and the siennas.
- **Mineral pigments** (which are also natural and inorganic) include vermilion (made from cinnabar/mercuric sulfide) and green malachite.
- **Artificial inorganic pigments** are produced rather than found, many created by ancient alchemists: verdigris, Naples yellow and sandarac.
- **Natural organic pigments**, also very old, are taken from plant or animal sources: Indian yellow (cow urine from India), sap green, and bone black (calcined bones).
- **Synthetic organic pigments** developed in the 19th century: indanthren and heliogen.

Toxic substances in pigments

- Antimony causes lung damage with longtime exposure.
- Lead causes anemia, gastrointestinal problems and damages peripheral nerves, kidneys, the reproductive system and the brain.

- Cadmium is very toxic when burned.
- Cobalt is harmful if inhaled or swallowed, with danger in cumulative effects.
- Copper is harmful if inhaled or swallowed.
- Mercury leads to poisoning and nerve damage with cumulative exposure.
- Nickel leads to nerve damage.
- Manganese leads to nerve damage.

Toxic pigments to avoid

Highly toxic pigments or probable carcinogens

- antimony white
- barium yellow
- burnt or raw umber
- cadmium yellow, red or orange
- cadmium barium colors
- chrome green, orange and yellow
- cobalt violet or yellow
- lead or flake white
- lithol red
- manganese violet
- molybdate orange
- Naples yellow
- strontium yellow
- vermilion
- zinc sulfide
- zinc yellow

Moderately or slightly toxic pigments

- alizarin crimson
- carbon black
- chromium oxide green
- cerulean blue
- cobalt blue
- cobalt green
- manganese blue
- Prussian blue
- toluidine red
- toluidine yellow
- viridian
- zinc white

Hazards of solvents and adhesives

Solvents are liquids (such as turpentine and mineral spirits) used for thinning and cleaning up oil-based paints. All solvents are hazardous and must be used with care and proper ventilation. In general, try to use water-soluble materials when possible and look for materials that are certified nontoxic by the Art and Craft Materials Institute.

- Solvents can cause defatting of the skin and dermatitis. Turpentine can cause skin allergies and be absorbed through the skin.
- Inhaling solvents can cause narcosis, which includes dizziness, headaches, drowsiness, nausea, fatigue, loss of coordination, respiratory irritation and coma.
- Chronic inhalation of solvents can cause decreased coordination, behavioral changes and brain damage. Chronic inhalation of turpentine can cause kidney damage, respiratory irritation and allergies. Odorless mineral spirits and turpenoid are less hazardous.
- Ingestion of turpentine or mineral spirits can be fatal.
- Traditional rubber cement is hazardous to inhale and should not be used.

More on artist safety

The following organizations and web sites provide information and guidelines for hazardous materials in the arts.

Health Hazards in the Arts: Information for Artists, Craftspeople and Photographers

Wallace Library, Rochester Institute of Technology
www.wally2.rit.edu/guides/healthhaz.html

Center for Safety in the Arts

www.artswire.org:70/1/csa

Safety checklist

The following list is adapted from "Checklist for Art Schools and Departments" by Michael McCann, Ph.D., of the Center for Safety in the Arts.

Toxics safety

- Use the least toxic materials available.
- Use water-based materials whenever possible.
- Use liquid products rather than powders that could be inhaled.
- Have adequate ventilation (open windows, exhaust fans, outdoor work space and so on) when working with hazardous materials.
- Don't eat, drink or smoke while working with art materials. When sanding, heating or spraying art materials, be careful not to inhale dust or fumes.
- Close all containers when not in use.
- Wet-mop floors rather than sweep them, to avoid raising hazardous dust.
- Clean up spills right away.
- Use goggles, respirators or dust masks whenever recommended for the material you're using.
- Wash your hands often and have a first-aid kit handy.
- Have a plan for emergency eye wash.
- Don't let children use hazardous materials.

Fire safety

- Store flammable materials properly to avoid fire.
- Keep floors and work surfaces free of flammable clutter.
- Keep a fire extinguisher in the studio and know how to use it.
- Dispose of oily rags in metal containers to avoid spontaneous combustion. Take them outside daily, and dispose of them properly. Trash containing oils, solvents and paints should not be put in ordinary garbage but taken to a hazardous materials recycling site (along with used batteries, used car oil and so on).
- Make sure any power tools are properly grounded and that wiring is adequate and safe.

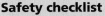

*There are
Six Essentials
in painting.
The first is called spirit;
the second, rhythm;
the third, thought,
the fourth, scenery;
the fifth, the brush,
and the last is the ink.*
—Ching Hao, *Notes on Brushwork*, 925 A.D.

Three Birds
India ink on paper, Janet Isaacs Ashford, 1993.

DRAWING INKS

Inks can be used with mechanical pens (such as Rapidograph) or with traditional dipping pens and nibs. Waterproof inks can also be floated on water to create patterns for marbling using the Suminogashi method.

Water-resistant ink. Black drawing ink (also called India ink) is made to be permanent when dry. A wash of watercolor or diluted ink can be painted over a dry ink drawing without smudging it.

Water-soluble ink. Water-soluble inks can be blurred with water after drying, which is sometimes desired.

Colored ink. Colored drawing inks vary in permanence. Look for brands that contain permanent pigments and are lightfast (resistant to fading).

Marker pens. These versatile pens, also called felt tip pens or markers, provide a convenient way to draw with vivid colored inks and come in a wide variety of sizes and tip shapes. They come in both water-soluble and water-resistant types, and in metallic inks.

CRAYONS

Traditionally, a crayon is any drawing substance that's in stick form. Crayons include chalk and pastel, Conté crayon, charcoal and wax.

Pastel and chalk. Both chalks and pastels are made of powdered pigments compressed with gum, with chalk being more tightly compressed and harder. Pastels come in hard and soft varieties, round or square shaped sticks, and in pencils. They leave a powdery surface which can be smudged to blend colors, then protected with a fixative (see "Spray coating" on page 76). Some pastels, called oil pastels, also contain oil, have a greasier texture and do not require protection with a fixative.

Conté crayon. Nicolas Jacques Conté invented this type of crayon in 1795 in France. Traditionally made of graphite and clay, today they're made of fabricated chalk and most commonly come in black, gray, white and red-brown. They're used especially for figure studies and sketching on colored papers.

Charcoal. Charcoal is made by binding wooden sticks together (from vines or willow branches) and baking them in an airtight oven so that they turn black but don't turn to ash. Charcoal produces a soft black mark and is used especially for life drawing and sketching.

Wax and oil. The type of crayons used by children are often made of pigment mixed with wax or oil. Crayola crayons are made with petroleum products but Prang crayons use renewable soybean oil as a binder. (For more information on Prang see "The Father of the American Greeting Card" on page 79).

Appreciating Paper

A finished drawing is always an interaction between the art medium—such as pencil or paint—and the "support." The most commonly used support in fine arts is paper, which holds true for digital arts as well. We take paper for granted, but before the 1400s Western artists used cumbersome wax tablets for sketching and used expensive parchment made from animal hides for permanent drawings. The introduction of paper made it possible for artists to make many rough sketches and compare them side by side! It provided a support for the new art of engraving and it also became the foundation of the newly developing printing industry. In other words, paper transformed the practice of art and literature in the West.

The history of paper

Historians believe that the first known papers were made of hemp fiber in China in the period from around 100 B.C. to 100 A.D. Papermaking spread from China to Korea in the sixth century A.D. and to Japan around 610 A.D. It was another 600 years before this technology reached Europe. Ancient Egyptians used papyrus (a form of paper made from the stems of rushes) while the ancient Romans wrote and drew on parchment made of dried sheep and goat skins. During the eighth century, the Chinese techniques of papermaking with plant fiber reached the Arab world and North Africa. North Africans brought papermaking to Spain in the twelfth century, and by the sixteenth century there were many mills in Europe producing handmade papers for drawing, writing and printing. For the first 300 years of papermaking in Europe, this versatile material was made of rags—worn out clothes made of hemp, flax and cotton. The first Gutenberg Bible and the first drafts of our Declaration of Independence were printed on hemp paper of this type. So for a long time paper has been primarily a recycled product, based on renewal resources (see "The Politics of Paper" on page 69).

HOW PAPER IS MADE

Paper is made of plant fibers which have been torn up and soaked in

Papermaking in the Renaissance
This woodcut of The Papermaker was made by Jost Amman and published in *The Book of Trades* (Ständebuch) in Germany in 1568. A reproduction was published with English translations by Dover Publications in 1973. The text reads: "The papermaker, in his water-driven mill, makes smooth white sheets of paper from rags that have been chopped up, soaked, placed on the sieve, pressed and dried."

One of the great basic inventions of mankind, as important for the growth of civilization as the discovery of the wheel or the firing of glass, paper is a fabulous material, diverse in qualities and adaptable in use. Rough and smooth, delicate and strong, prized and despised— on it Shakespeare wrote sonnets and Dürer drew praying hands, while the fishmonger wraps cod in it for which the housewife will pay in paper currency. In the Welsh village where I was born, because they were poor, the men used to have special suits for funerals made of a shiny, carbon-black paper like the end papers in their nonconformist hymnbooks.

—Trevor Thomas, from the foreword to *Creating with Paper: Basic Forms and Variations* by Pauline Johnson (University of Washington Press, 1958; reprinted by Dover Publications, 1991)

Rags make paper,
Paper makes money,
Money makes banks,
Banks make loans,
Loans make beggars,
Beggars make rags.

—Author unknown, circa eighteenth century,
quoted in *Papermaking: The History and*
Technique of an Ancient Craft, Dard Hunter
(Knopf, 1947; Dover, 1978)

Decorative paper
A selection of decorative and artist papers including
red tissue with metallic texture, watercolor paper,
paper printed with an arts and crafts era pattern,
marbled paper and miscellaneous flecked and
textured papers.

Paper for fine art

There are many types of paper used for fine art work, varying in thickness, brightness, color and texture. Art paper is sold in pads, notebooks and loose sheets in several standard sizes ranging from 9 by 12 inches to 19 by 24 inches. Papers meant for sketching and school crafts (newsprint, construction paper, butcher paper) are made of wood pulp. Better quality papers are machine-made of linen and cotton rags. The best art papers are handmade and usually come in large sheets that can be cut to size for specific uses.

PAPER FOR DRAWING AND PAINTING

Sketching and drawing paper. Letter-sized office paper sold in reams is the cheapest and most available type of paper for sketching. Art supply stores also sell newsprint and heavier, whiter sketching and drawing papers in many sizes. These papers are good for use with pencils but may be too rough for ink pens and too thin or porous for paint.

Layout and visualizing paper. This paper is semitransparent, does not bleed through and is good for sketching with felt-tip markers.

Watercolor paper, available in sheets, boards, pads and blocks, is highly textured and made either by machine or by hand in whites, creams and colors. It's excellent for use with watercolor, pastel, colored pencil and gouache. The Arches paper mill in the Lorraine region of France has been producing 100 percent cotton, mould-made watercolor papers since 1492!

HEAVIER PAPERS AND BOARDS

Bristol board, with its smooth, coated surface, makes a good support for pen and ink and for colored pencil work. It can also be used with gouache.

Foam core board. This stiff type of poster board consists of a layer of foam about a quarter inch thick, with coated paperboard on both sides. It's excellent for mounting art work and for posters and exhibits.

Card or cardboard. This stiffer paper, in varying thicknesses, is made of pressed paper pulp or adhered sheets of paper. It's used for mounting and for various types of "cards," such as greeting cards, postcards, business cards, playing cards, and so on.

Making paper at school

A close-up of paper containing shredded newspaper and potpourri, made at Skyline Elementary School in Solana Beach, California by Molly Ashford, with her third-grade teacher Bobbie Hilton, 1994.

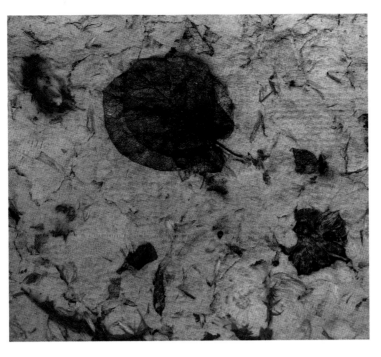

Making Your Own Paper

Paper can be made at home using scrap paper torn into small bits. The scraps are soaked in water until soft, mixed in a kitchen blender, poured into a dishpan and then scooped up with a screen stretched over a wooden frame (deckle). Inexpensive deckles and molds can be made from canvas stretchers (sold at art supply stores) or from embroidery hoops.

Handmade paper can be decorated with leaves and flowers, glitter or other small thin objects. Paper made in this way will probably be too thick and fragile to be printed with a desktop printer, but it can be used as a support or background for computer printed graphics or type, which can be attached with glue or other fasteners.

Many art supply stores sell paper-making kits with instructions. In addition, the books listed below contain good instructions for making handmade paper with household tools.

Art and Craft of Handmade Paper
Vance Studley
Dover Publications, 1990

The Art of Papermaking
Bernard Toale
Davis Publications, 1983

Bookworks: Making Books by Hand
Gwenyth Swain
with the Minnesota Center for Book Arts
Carolrhoda Books, 1995

Creative Handmade Paper: How to Make Paper from Recycled and Natural Materials
David Watson
Search Press, 1991

SPECIALTY PAPERS

Tissue paper is thin, strong, pliable, translucent and available in many colors. It's especially suited for collage and can be adhered to regular paper using diluted glue or liquid starch.

Parchment and vellum. Parchment was originally made of the dried, stretched skins of sheep or goats, while vellum was made from calf bellies. Today, papers that imitate the translucence and irregularities of these materials are machine-made of plant fibers.

Glassine is thin, dense, and translucent. It resists air and dirt and so is often used to preserve or separate other sheets of paper. It makes especially charming see-through envelopes or overlay sheets.

Sandpaper. The grainy texture of fine arts sandpaper helps to hold pastel pigment in place.

DECORATIVE PAPERS

Handmade paper. Handmade decorative papers often include textural elements such as leaves and flower petals. These beautiful papers come in a wide variety of colors, textures and thicknesses and are used in bookbinding, collage and fine arts.

Paste paper is decorated by covering a sheet with a layer of paint or colored wheat paste and then raking through the paint with comb-like tools, something like finger painting.

Printed papers. Papers with printed patterns are often used for origami (paper folding) as well as for gift wrapping and collage.

Marbled paper. Hand-marbled papers are traditionally used as end papers in bookbinding.

Which Adhesive is Best?

Adhesives have various properties that determine which ones are best for different materials. Questions to ask about an adhesive include:

- How long does it take to dry?
- Is the bond flexible or will it crack?
- Can the dried adhesive be dissolved with water or not?
- Will it cause the paper to buckle or stretch?
- How long can it be stored without spoiling?

Tips for gluing and pasting

- Test adhesives with small samples of the paper you'll be using, to see how the materials work together.
- Let glued items dry overnight before using; if possible, place them under weights such as heavy books.
- Protect glued items from seeping glue or stickiness by placed sheets of waxed paper over them or between sheets.

There is mass production, but there can be no mass creation. The craftsperson proceeds by methods different from the machine.

—Victor Hammer from *Victor Hammer: An Artist's Testament*, 1988

Using Adhesives

Adhesives are used to attach things to each other. The adhesives described here are the ones commonly used to glue papers together or to glue paper to other surfaces such as wood and plastic. Remember that some adhesives are toxic (such as rubber cement) so check package labels for information.

Types of paste and glue

PASTE

Flour paste. Traditional homemade paste can be made from wheat or rice flour or cornstarch mixed with water. It's archival but must be refrigerated when wet.

Yamato Sticking Paste. This paste doesn't wrinkle thin tissue paper.

GLUE

White glue. Inexpensive white glue is a mainstay of craft work and can be used with wood, paper, leather and fabric. Too much can cause paper to buckle, so apply it thinly. Look for liquid glues that have the "AP Nontoxic" label, especially when they'll be used by children.

Glue pens and rollers. Liquid glue is available in pens and rollers that dispense glue through an applicator.

Glue stick. These easy-to-apply semi-solid glues come in twist-up dispensers and are especially handy for making greeting cards and for artist book work. Look for nontoxic, acid-free brands.

Memory Mount. This best-seller for scrap book work is nontoxic, repositionable, acid-free and archival quality.

PVA. Polyvinyl acetate is pH-neutral, makes a strong, long-lasting bond and is the first choice for bookbinding, box-making and collage. It can also be used to glue plastics together.

Re-lick glue. A brush-on or roll-on adhesive that can be remoistened after drying. Use for adding a strip of adhesive to handmade envelopes

Other adhesives

ADHESIVE TAPES AND SHEETS

Double-sided tape. Cellophane tape that's sticky on both sides can be used for mounting or attaching one piece of paper to another. It's also available with foam between the sticky surfaces to lift attached objects off the surface a little.

Mounting adhesive. Available in sheets or tape, sticky on both sides, mounting adhesive can be used to turn anything into a sticker and can be applied to both paper and cloth.

MOUNTING SQUARES AND STRIPS

Adhesive backed mounting squares. Sticky on both sides, these can be used to attach papers to each other or to attach lightweight papers (such as posters) to a wall.

Velcro. Adhesive backed velcro, in small squares, circles and strips, can be used to close folders and envelopes or stick items to each other, such as to mount a small item to a card (for example, a piece of candy, a crayon or a shell).

SPRAY ADHESIVES

These apply a thin, even coating of adhesive, but are hazardous to use, require adequate ventilation and are harmful to the environment. It's best to avoid using them.

Basic Craft Tools

It's good to have a box for storing basic arts and crafts tools, so everything is together in one place. Just the sight of the box and tools can be inspiring.

Folding and scoring

BONE FOLDER

This versatile tool is made of smoothed animal bone and is used for folding and scoring paper, especially in book arts. It's similar to a letter opener—with a pointed end and a blunt, rounded end—but is heftier. Use it to make smooth folds for greeting cards and origami, to score a fold line before folding or to burnish down glued papers.

Cutting and punching

SELF-HEALING CUTTING MAT

These special mats have a semi-hard plastic surface that heals itself after being cut. Use them as a protective table surface when cutting paper with razors and craft knives. They come in several different sizes, from 9- by 12-inch to 24- by 36-inch, and are marked with ruler grid lines.

KNIVES AND BLADES

Craft knife. The most well-known of this type are made by X-Acto and include many sizes of removable blades that fit into a metal or plastic stylus. Swivel knives are used for cutting curves. *Utility knife.* Used for cutting thicker materials such as mat board, this kind of knife uses replaceable blades.

Single edged razor blades can be used alone for cutting. To scrape glass, they can be inserted into a metal holder available at hardware stores.

Paper cutters have a long cutting blade hinged to a wood or plastic platform and are used for making straight cuts to trim paper. They range in size and quality and cost from around $35 to over $700. Office-supply and stationery stores sell serviceable models. Higher quality types are available from suppliers for fine arts and book binding.

STRAIGHT EDGES AND RULERS

Rulers are used for measuring, as guides for drawing straight lines, as edges when cutting with a craft knife and for tearing paper. Metal rulers are best for cutting and tearing while see-through plastic rulers are handy for measuring and marking. Rulers can be marked in inches, centimeters and/or picas.

SCISSORS

Scissors come in many sizes, both pointed and blunt. It's handy to have several sizes, including a small, sharp pair for making precise cuts for collage work and book binding.

Cutting Safely with a Craft Knife

The razors used in craft knives are sharp, so be careful and follow these simple rules.

- A dull blade is your enemy. You'll end up using too much pressure, which can cause your knife to slip. Change blades often, as soon as you notice any dullness or difficulty in cutting. A fresh, sharp blade will also avoid tearing the paper.
- Apply firm but moderate pressure with the knife. When cutting thicker papers or board or when cutting through a stack of papers, make several strokes at moderate pressure rather than try to cut through with one hard stroke.
- Use a metal ruler as a cutting guide and keep it between your knife and your fingers.
- When cutting curves, keep your fingers out of the path of the knife.

Essential tools
A bone folder, craft knife with replaceable blades and self-healing cutting mat are the tools I use most often for making cards, crafts and bookbinding.

DECKLE EDGE SCISSORS AND RULERS

Handmade papers have a characteristic torn-looking edge called a deckle edge (see "How Paper is Made" on page 67). Deckle edge rulers have a wavy edge that's used for tearing paper to imitate the traditional look. Deckle edge scissors (or paper edgers) have patterned blades that can create a variety of decorative edges, from zigzags to curves to deckles.

DECORATIVE HOLE PUNCHES

Use these tools to punch hearts, stars, snowflakes, trees, butterflies, moons and other shapes. Use the punched hole as a negative space (by layering it over a contrasting color); use the punched out piece in confetti or paste it onto another surface.

Tracing

PAPERS FOR TRACING

Tracing paper. Available in sheets, pads and rolls, the heavier weights (sometimes called vellum) can be used with pen and ink.

Matte acetate. Acetate is more transparent than tracing paper and the matte surface provides adherence for ink. Acetate can be cut to use as a template.

PAPERS FOR TRANSFERRING PATTERNS

Graphite transfer paper. Similar to carbon paper, this paper is covered with a layer of graphite and is used to transfer drawings from paper to another surface, such as canvas.

Chalk paper. Paper coated with light-colored chalk is used to transfer drawings onto dark-colored papers.

LIGHT BOXES

A light box has a translucent plastic surface with a light source underneath. It can be used for viewing slides and also makes tracing easier. Place the graphic to be traced on the light box, place plain paper over it, turn on the light and trace.

OVERHEAD PROJECTORS

This type of projector is placed on small flat art work (such as a drawing) that's on a horizontal surface and enlarges and projects it onto a vertical surface (such as a stretched canvas) onto which the image is traced.

Protecting

LAMINATING

Lamination is often applied to protect art work that will be used often or to create place mats or coasters. The Xyron company makes a number of different hand-cranked machines that apply lamination material or archival adhesive or both, without electricity or heat. Some of the Xyron series can also apply magnet film to any paper or cloth, simply by cranking it through the machine. (For a project made with the Xyron 510 see "Using Lamination" on page 119.)

SPRAY COATING

Various types of protective coatings are available in aerosol cans, including fixative (for protecting art made with pastels, for example), clear gloss, matte finish and varnish. Most of these sprays are hazardous to inhale. Check cans for the certified "AP Nontoxic" label. It's best to find alternatives to aerosol cans containing chemicals that deplete our planet's ozone layer.

Stamping and embossing

RUBBER STAMPS

Rubber stamps are available in a vast array of decorative images, symbols and alphabets. All can be used to embellish computer-made designs and prints. Stamps can be used with both water-soluble and water-resistent inks, in a wide range of colors and multi-color stamp pads. In addition, wet stamp impressions can be sprinkled with embossing powder, which is then dried with a heat gun to produce a slightly raised, often metallic effect. Remember that the designs on decorative rubber stamps are copyrighted, though some rubber-stamp suppliers allow craftspeople to sell items that have been handmade using their rubber stamps, without requesting copyright permission. These are called "angel" companies.

EMBOSSING TOOLS

In addition to the embossing powders used with rubber stamping, there are various tools used to emboss paper directly—that is, to create an image by making indentations. These small presses are available in various symbols and letters.

A jumble of stamps
This test paper was made using stamps supplied by Retro Rubber Stamps (see Resources section). Before stamping on expensive paper, it's a good idea to first stamp on scrap paper, to check ink coverage and possible clogging. Your test paper may later become part of a collage or other art project.

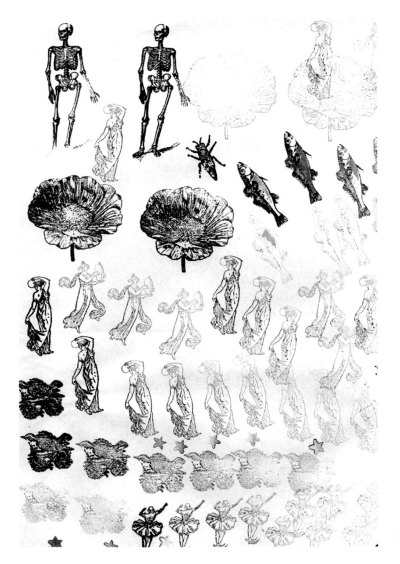

Your Basic Art Kit

Here is a list of the artist tools I use most often. With this equipment you will be able to create most of the projects in this book. (Also see the listing of computer and software tools in "Your Digital Toolbox" on page 25.)

Tools
- self-healing cutting mat
- craft knife and replacement blades
- metal ruler
- clear plastic ruler with grid lines
- bone folder
- liquid white glue or PVA
- glue sticks
- sharp scissors
- paper cutter
- hole punch
- needles and thread

Materials
- computer printable papers
- decorative papers
- pads of drawing paper
- watercolor paper
- assorted office and decorative stickers
- assorted envelopes and folders
- waxed paper
- scratch paper

Art media
- set of dry gouache paints
- set of acrylic paints in tubes
- box of colored pencils
- set of colored felt tip marker pens
- bottle of India ink
- bottles of colored ink
- ink pen nibs and holder
- assorted paint brushes in various sizes
- assorted pencils and ball point pens
- assorted rubber stamps
- stamp pads in black and colors

I store my materials on shelves in a workroom. Smaller papers are stored flat and larger decorative papers are hung over a dowel suspended from the ceiling. To organize smaller items I use a variety of containers including tin cans, glass jars, baskets, shoe boxes, other small packing boxes and see-through plastic boxes with dividers (sold in craft and office supply stores).

5 Making Cards and Small Books

CORRESPONDENCE BETWEEN FRIENDS and relatives has been an important part of European and American life for as long as there have been reliable postal systems. The first postal station in the United States was established at a tavern in Boston in 1639. In 1775 Benjamin Franklin was named the first Postmaster General under the Continental Congress. The first American postage stamps were issued in 1847 and the first street letterboxes appeared in 1858.

Letters between famous persons are often collected and published to provide insight into the development of ideas, while correspondence between ordinary people provides an eyewitness account of history. People have written fewer letters since the invention of the telephone, and since these conversations are rarely recorded, this form of audio correspondence is lost to history. E-mail correspondence has revived the practice of writing, but in a less tangible and personal form than letters written on paper. Today a handwritten letter or card is a rare and highly valued form of communication.

The History of Stationery and Cards

In addition to letters written on letter sheets, the development of the greeting card made it possible to send pictures as well as words to friends and relatives. The first printed Christmas card was designed by Sir Henry Cole (a.k.a. Felix Summerly), a writer and publisher of books and journals on art and design. In 1843, having no time to write Christmas letters to all his contacts, he asked artist John Calcott Horsley to illustrate a Christmas dinner scene and had it printed with the message "A Merry Christmas and A Happy New Year to You." This began the custom of sending printed cards on holidays. The low cost of postage meant that by the 1870s even working class English people could afford to buy and

Dearest, it's been a long time since

Janet Ashford
10277 Nichols Lane

Writing a letter
Hand-written letters are a treasure. This card was made by printing an illustration from *Books, Reading and Writing Illustrations: CD-ROM and Book* (Dover, 1998) onto a piece of flecked paper and using decorative edge scissors to embellish the edge. Starting the letter on the front leads the reader to open the card.

send cards. Americans relied on imported cards until 1874, when Louis Prang produced the first American Christmas card and launched the American greeting card industry.

Types of cards

Today the novelty of color printing has worn off and mass-produced greeting cards are no longer as charming and "collectible" as they once were. A handmade card is truly rare and appreciated. Use the following list of categories as a guide to the many occasions that warrant a handmade card:

- Anniversaries
- Bas/Bar Mitzvah
- Birth Announcements
- Birthdays
- Christmas
- Easter
- Get Well Soon
- Graduations
- Hanukkah
- Humor
- Kwanza
- Love & Romance
- Party Invitations
- Sympathy
- Thank You
- Valentine's Day

Holiday symbols
Ancient pagan rites of tree worship survive in the European and American Christmas custom of a holiday tree. This Victorian era illustration is from *Full-Color Decorative Christmas Illustrations: CD-ROM and Book* (Dover, 1999).

The Father of the American Greeting Card

Louis Prang was a talented and hard-working man who distinguished himself by advancing the art of color printing, by creating the American greeting card industry and by introducing art education into schools. Prang was born in 1824 in Breslau, Silesia (now Poland). His father ran a fabric printing factory in Bohemia (part of Austria) and Louis studied printing and dyeing techniques there before emigrating as a political refugee to America in 1850. He settled in Boston and established a color printing press, further developing the technique of chromolithography. In addition to printing textbooks, art reproductions, maps, cigar labels and business "trade cards," Prang also printed "scrap"— collectible colorful album cards of nostalgic Victorian-style flowers, butterflies, birds, animals and children. These "beautiful art bits" were avidly collected and displayed in albums (called "scrap books").

Prang has also been called "The Father of the American Christmas Card," producing the first one in 1874. Card designs for Easter, the New Year, Valentine's Day and birthdays soon followed. Prang held national competitions for card designs and verse. His greeting cards, as with all his color printing, were created from up to 25 separate printing stones, all perfectly aligned. It might take months for a dozen artists to prepare the stones, costing up to $6,000 (in 1870s dollars) to create one card. Once the work was done, however, many thousands of cards could be printed. The cards were highly prized and it is said that young women of the time would record in their diaries how many "Prangs" they had received. Prang's work helped to make good quality color reproductions affordable for the average American.

Unrestrained by the limitations of the letterpress and hundreds of years of type and graphic design history, the designers of chromolithography art sometimes ran riot, distorting type and creating florid color art. By the 1890s however, photo processes began to replace chromolithography. Prang merged his firm with a photo process printer in 1897, ensuring his continued success. But his famous competitors, Currier and Ives, continued using chromolithography to print sentimental designs and went bankrupt soon after 1900.

Louis Prang was also an innovator in artist materials and education. When Prang began teaching art to his daughter in 1856 he found it hard to get good-quality, non-toxic materials. So he formulated his own safe crayons and watercolor sets and contracted with the American Crayon Company to manufacture them. Prang also developed and published art instruction books, helping to establish the teaching of art in America's public schools. He often donated art materials to schools that were starting up the teaching of art, which had previously been available only to the wealthy. Prang's art supplies are still sold by the Dixon Ticonderoga Company, which recently introduced crayons made entirely of soybean oil rather than petroleum products.

Louis Prang died in 1909 at the age of 85. His name is engraved on the base of the Statue of Liberty along with other immigrants who made great contributions to the United States. In Boston there is a Louis Prang Street near the Museum of Fine Arts.

For a history of Prang's work see the Dixon Ticonderoga Company web site at www.prang.com/prang/louisprang/

Victorian art in America
An idealized illustration of babies, one of thousands of sentimental Victorian images printed in the late 1800s by American innovator Louis Prang.

Evolution of a greeting card
Beautiful fruit trees in bloom attracted my eye as I walked through the village of Mendocino in April. I took a close-up shot with my digital camera, then converted the photo to grayscale and used Unsharp Mask to exaggerate the edges. I printed the black-and-white image on my laser printer, placed tracing paper over it and made a pencil drawing, taking some liberties with the placement of the flowers. This drawing became the basis for various card illustrations. For a full shot of the fruit trees, see page 21.

Creating Greeting Card Designs

Paper for making cards

Card-weight paper is best for greeting cards, as it is stiff and thick enough to stand up when folded. Designs can be printed directly on card stock, then cut to size (if necessary) and folded. In addition, some suppliers provide inkjet and laser greeting card paper that is already sized, scored and perforated. Card stock is available in a variety of colors and textures. White or very pale colors are best for printing color images, but black-and-white images can be printed on brightly colored card stock.

Printing in black-and-white

Black-and-white clip art is an inspiring source of designs for greeting cards. An old engraving printed on a slightly textured, cream-colored paper looks elegant all by itself. But there are many ways to add touches of color to cards printed in black ink only. You can print on colored paper, add stickers or stamps, hand-color the printed art with colored pencil or paint, or use colored envelopes.

Printing in color

Color art derived from photos, scans and color clip art can be printed directly onto white card stock, which can then be cut and folded. But you may want to print several copies of your color art on a single sheet of photo quality paper, cut them out and paste them onto folded cards made of more interesting handmade, textured or colored paper.

Greeting card art in black-and-white and color
To create a black-and-white greeting card illustration in a horizontal format, I looked for geometric clip art that would contrast with the curving lines of my flower drawing. I found just the right frame in *Persian Ceramic Designs* (Stemmer House, 1983), scanned it, removed the material inside the frame and pasted in a scan of my pencil drawing.

To create a version in a vertical format I combined the scanned drawing with a hand-drawn border and a leaf ornament taken from 1500 *Decorative Ornaments: CD-ROM and Book* (Dover, 2000).

To create color versions of both illustrations I used Streamline to autotrace each black-and-white drawing, thus converting it from a bitmapped TIFF to PostScript art. I then used Illustrator to add color gradients.

Printing in black-and-white and color

Black-and-white art can be printed on white or colored paper and combined with colored envelopes and hand-painted touches to create a colorful effect. To create the colored card at left, I printed the same black line image on three pieces of differently colored paper, cut out sections and pasted them on top of each other.

Color art can be printed on white card stock (below, card in back) or on photo-quality paper which is then cut out and pasted onto a colored card. Photo paper will often produce a crisper image. It's also possible to print color images on light colored paper, such as yellow, which will impart an interesting color cast to the art.

I printed my card designs in two sizes to match envelopes available in 5-inch by 7-inch size (A7) and 4 $\frac{1}{4}$-inch by 5 $\frac{1}{2}$-inch size (Baronial or invitation). For details on printing to match envelopes see page 86.

Creative Card Techniques

There are many ways to use hand-work techniques to make computer-printed images richer and less "computery." In addition, all of the techniques shown here for greeting cards can also be used to create larger prints and art for framing. For more ideas, look at books dealing with traditional paper craft and decoration. Techniques can often be adapted to computer crafting, using computer printed output as part of the project.

Embellish the surface

DRAW AND PAINT

Draw or paint on printed images using watercolor, gouache, colored pencil, marking pens or pastels. You can work in coloring-book fashion by adding color to the white spaces in black-and-white designs or by painting over sections of color scans or photos, perhaps adding mustaches or funny hats to favorite people.

USE RUBBER STAMPS

Stamp on top of printed output with rubber stamps and colored inks. You can also try scanning stamped designs or the stamps themselves and blowing these up to use as background textures.

USE STICKERS

Add ready-made stickers as accents or borders or try creating your own custom stickers by printing on a pre-cut sticker sheet.

ADD GLITTER AND SHINE

Brush glue onto a computer print and then sprinkle with glitter. Also try drawing on prints with gold or silver metallic ink pens or with sparkly gel pens. This is especially effective on prints with rich, dark colors.

Adding color to black-and-white prints
I made a laser print of a scanned engraving and added unexpected color using felt tip pens. I then cut out the figure and placed it over two pieces of decorative paper—a scrap with a metallic print and, above it, a circling design created by my two daughters. (They had put a piece of paper on an old turn table and spun it while holding pens to the surface.) The unusual choice of colors and textures acts as a contrast to the sentimentality of the old engraving. The card was finished with metallic star stickers. The image was scanned from *Love and Romance: A Pictorial Archive from Nineteenth-Century Sources* (Dover, 1989).

Printing on decorative paper
To create a birthday card I scanned an early 20th century Italian astrological drawing from *Treasury of Book Ornament and Decoration* (Dover, 1986). I printed the symbol and the "Happy Birthday!" text on a piece of light-colored marbled paper, cut out these pieces and pasted them onto a piece of darker marbled paper in the same red-brown hues. The papers were hand-marbled using acrylic paints floated on traditional Irish Moss gel. For instructions on the easier Suminogashi method of marbling with inks floated on water see *Creative Paper Art: Techniques for Transforming the Surface* by Nancy Welch (Sterling, 1999).

Experiment with papers

PRINT ON DECORATIVE PAPER

Print on hand-decorated paper—such as marbled paper—or paper that's been lightly painted with watercolor washes. Make sure the paper is light enough to allow your printed design to show clearly.

PRINT ON CLEAR FILM

Try printing on clear transparency film, either in color or black-and-white, and then overlay the film onto decorative paper backgrounds.

Layering with transparency
A page of Chinese text caught my eye in the Encore Exotica collection from Apple Tree Lane (see Resources). Following the Chinese theme, I pasted a piece of orange and gold Joss paper at the top of a folded card and a scrap of torn blue handmade paper at the bottom. I then scanned the text and printed it on Ink Jet Transparency Film from RoyalBrites. I cut the printed film, folded the top and bottom edges and slid it over the card, fastening the edges on the inside with gold foil stickers and punching a single staple through the center. I then removed a gold foil medallion from a package of Chinese soap and pasted it over the staple. The result is an interesting blend of Asian scraps.

USE FOUND PAPER

Use found paper—such as pages of text from old books and magazines— as background elements in card designs. Pages in foreign languages are especially charming and less distracting than English. (For ideas see "Using Found Paper" on page 68.)

Cut and paste computer prints

Computer prints can be cut up into pieces and pasted on top of each other or next to each other to create designs. Here are some ideas:

COMBINE TWO VERSIONS OF THE SAME IMAGE

Print one image in focus and the same image out of focus. Cut the focussed one into strips and paste on the other.

CREATE A QUILT DESIGN

Print several pages of scanned textures. Cut the prints into geometrical shapes and paste the pieces together into a traditional quilt design.

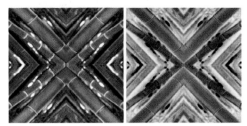

Creating a paper quilt design
I started by scanning a photo of bamboo taken at the Quail Botanical Gardens in Encinitas, California. I used Photoshop to rotate the photo 45 degrees, selected a square near the center, and pasted it into a new document where I made three copies of the square and rotated them so they all pointed toward the center. I then converted the grid design to a negative image and increased the saturation of the reds. I printed the altered scan, cut it into four pieces and pasted them onto a piece of decorative red paper that was attached to a card. I added pieces of gold paper as accents.

Cutting a window
The richly detailed cover of this card was scanned from *Treasury of Illuminated Borders in Full Color* (Dover, 1988). I printed it on photo quality matte paper and used glue stick to attach it to a sheet of card stock with a glossy light brown coating on one side. I then used an X-Acto knife with a sharp new blade to cut away the white space in the center of the border. I pasted a piece of brown decorative paper on the inside of the card and over that pasted a school photo of my daughter Molly.

Using small objects
To create the background art for this card I made a close-up scan of an actual bluebird feather and boosted its color saturation in Photoshop. A color print of the scan was pasted onto a blue card along with a piece of decorative paste paper from Maziarczyk Paperworks, a torn piece of handmade red paper and the cut half of a gold medallion sticker. Two small blackbird feathers were then attached to the card using gold and silver metallic embroidery thread.

COMBINE COLORED PAPERS

Print the same image on two or more different colors of paper. Cut each print into pieces, then reassemble into one image using pieces from each color.

BREAK AN IMAGE INTO PIECES

Cut a single image into pieces and paste them back down on a decorative background paper with gaps between them.

Add decorative elements

ADD BOWS AND TIES

Tie decorative bows of ribbon, cord, embroidery thread or raffia.

ATTACH SMALL OBJECTS

Attach a small object such as a dried flower or leaf, a sea shell, a piece of candy or a feather. Use glue or ties to fasten the object, or velcro tabs or two-sided tape if the object should be removable. Try scanning a close-up of the object to print as a background for the card to which it will be attached. Experiment with applying digital filters to alter the image.

ADD DECORATIONS

Use glue stick or other adhesive to attach small pieces of decorative paper, doilies, paper leaves, bits of lace, ribbon or cloth. Larger pieces can be used as backgrounds.

Cut and fold

CUT A WINDOW

Print a border on a card, or print it on photo paper and glue to a card. Carefully use a craft knife to cut a window through the card. Mount a photo or other art print on the inside of the card, to be seen through the window.

MAKE DECORATIVE EDGES

Create a decorative edge by tearing or cutting with deckle-edge scissors or by punching with a decorative hole punch or corner punch.

STITCH AND SEW

Use the decorative stitches on a sewing machine or stitch or embroider by hand using needle-and-thread. Try stitching a simple blanket stitch around the edges of card, reminiscent of the sewing cards that children use.

MAKE FOLDS

Make folds or score curved lines into a card using a bone folder. Try making a card that can stand up like a Japanese shoji panel screen.

DISTRESS COMPUTER PRINTS

Distress printed output by crumpling it, folding it many times, singeing its edges, wetting it or staining it.

MAKE A CUT-PAPER DESIGN

Scan a simple black-and-white design, fill shapes with solid black as needed, print on colored paper and cut away the black areas. Layer the cut paper over a contrasting color paper.

Creating a "scrapbook page" card

To create a series of greeting cards for my daughter Molly, I chose various Victorian images of her favorites—cats, butterflies and flowers— from *500 Full-Color Decorative Illustrations: CD-ROM and Book* (Dover, 2000) and arranged them in PageMaker over a background oval and rectangle in complementary pastel colors. Screen shots from PageMaker show four of the compositions. I printed the cards with Molly's name and address on the back.

Combining techniques

To create a Valentine card I started by scanning a paper doily from RoyalBrites and saved it as a bitmap. I then imported it into PageMaker and layered two copies, coloring one red and the other pink. I printed the doilies on pink paper and folded it to create the card. I then used glue stick to attach a RoyalBrites red heart doily to the front of the card and placed a sticker in the center. The inside of the card contains two sheets, which are sewn into the card fold with metallic thread using a pamphlet stitch (see page 94). The inner red sheet contains a poem while the outer pink sheet is printed with a Victorian valentine illustration and is trimmed with decorative-edge scissors.

Creating a folded card

I printed the koi art created for Chapter 2 (see "'Tracing' Over Photo References" on page 29) on matte photo paper and used glue stick to paste it onto a decorative green card made of handmade paper from Nepal (Lami Li Stationery imported by Savoir-Faire). I then made extra folds to create a six-panel card that looks like a small Japanese folding screen.

Setting Up Cards for Standard Envelope Sizes

The envelopes most commonly available in stationery and office supply stores include the following, all of which can be used with cards and letter sheets printed on 8 ½ by 11-inch paper. Make sure that your cards are cut to be about one quarter inch smaller in height and width than the size of the envelope.

A2 or #5 ½
- 4 ⅜ by 5 ¾ inches
- Also called Baronial, Invitation or Announcement envelopes
- Fits a letter size sheet folded twice into four sections; or cut in half, each half folded once; or cut in half twice into four separate unfolded cards

A7
- 5 ¼ by 7 ¼ inches
- Fits a 10 by 7-inch card, folded once to 5 by 7-inch size

#10 Regular Business size
- 4 ⅛ by 9 ½ inches
- Fits a letter size sheet folded twice into three sections

#6 ¾ Small letter size
- 3 ⅝ by 6 ½ inches
- Fits a letter size sheet folded three times into six sections

Setting up cards in A7 format

A common size for greeting cards is 5 by 7 inches, which fits into an A7 envelope. Card designs can be printed on letter-size sheets and then trimmed to 10 by 7 inches after printing. I used PageMaker to set up the cards below. For cards that will be trimmed from a letter-size sheet, I position my image and text in the upper left hand corner of the page, so that only two cuts with my paper cutter are required to trim the printed sheet. But for images that should bleed (extend beyond the edges of the card) I position the card in the upper center of the sheet and make three cuts to trim it. The cutting lines are indicated.

Setting up a letter sheet

To create a letter-size sheet to fit a business-size or small letter-size envelope, I positioned a border and my name and address at the top of an 8½ by 11-inch page. (The border was created by copying and reflecting the leaf motif from my vertical flower art.)

A7, horizontal format

A7, vertical format

A7, horizontal format with bleed

Letter-size sheet

Setting up cards in A2 format

This 5 ½-inch by 4 ¼-inch size is often used for invitations and thank-you notes and works well for greeting cards as well. This format makes full use of letter-size sheets with no wasted paper. Printed sheets are cut in half once, either vertically or horizontally, and folded once to create the card.

Printing multiples

Sometimes I prefer to print several copies of my card art on good quality photo paper and cut and paste them onto cards made of textured paper.

Setting up a small letter

For a smaller sheet to fit an A2 envelope I use a decorative border, positioned two copies of it with my name and address, then cut the printed sheet in half.

Baronial, horizontal format

Baronial, vertical format

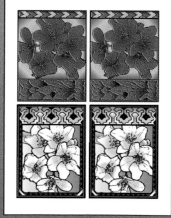

Greeting card art printed 4 up

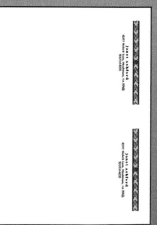

Small letter sheets

Working with Envelopes

Using ready-made envelopes

The most convenient way to provide envelopes for computer-generated stationery is to use ready-made envelopes in standard sizes and create greeting cards and note cards sized to fit them. This approach lets you concentrate your creative energy on the card and complement it in a simple way with a plain envelope in white or a matching color. See page 81 for examples of this approach. For guidelines see "Setting Up Cards for Standard Envelope Sizes" on the opposite page.

Printing custom envelopes

Though it takes more time, it's exciting to cut and fold an envelope from paper you've printed with photos or artwork. Outlines of envelopes can be printed on thick paper and cut out to make templates, or can be scanned and used as guides in an image-editing program. See "Using Envelope Templates" on page 88.

Custom printed envelopes

To create a pair of special envelopes I used the same digital photo and Illustrator artwork used to create the greeting cards shown on page 81. The small screen shots show how I superimposed one of my Baronial envelope templates onto the Illustrator drawing and onto the photo.

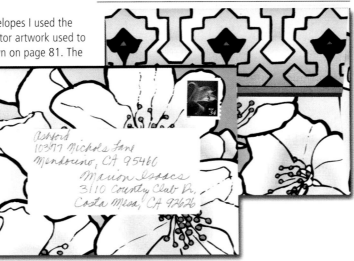

Addressing a custom envelope

An envelope made from a printed image can be too densely colored to allow space for an address. I worked around this in two ways. On the flower drawing envelope I added a white address label. On the flower photo envelope I used Photoshop to select a triangular area and lighten it to create a writing space.

Sealing Envelopes

There are several ways to fasten handmade envelopes.

Glue and paste

The bottom flap can be attached to the two side flaps most easily using glue stick. The top flap can also be glued, if you're planning to send the envelope sealed. But if the envelope is part of a gift set of stationery, you can apply "re-lick" glue to the edges of the top flap. This is a brush-on or roll-on adhesive that can be re-moistened after drying. In addition, Scotch makes a non-toxic product called Restickable Adhesive Glue Stick.

Stickers

After gluing the bottom part of an envelope together, the top flap can be easily and attractively fastened down with a decorative sticker or seal. Embossed metallic seals are especially elegant.

Buttons

Buttons can be sewn onto the top flap and the bottom part of an envelope and then wrapped with thin cord to close, just as interoffice memo envelopes are often closed by wrapping string around two disks. In addition to using pretty buttons from your button box, you can contact Fascinating Folds (see Resources) for decorative paper buttons.

Sealing wax

Many art supply stores still sell old-fashioned sealing wax which comes in a stick with a wick like that of a candle. Light the wick with a match, drip the hot wax onto the envelope, then press down the cooling wax with a metal stamp.

Using Envelope Templates

One of the easiest ways to create a template for making an envelope is to carefully open a ready-made envelope and scan it. That's what I did to create the four templates on the opposite page. After scanning four different envelopes at 100%, I placed each scan in Illustrator and used the pen tool to draw around the edges. Each envelope can be printed on a letter-size sheet. Here's how you can use the templates:

1. Scanning the templates

Scan the opposite page, enlarging to 160 percent so that each envelope page outline equals 8 1/2 inches by 11 inches. (The templates are printed here at 40 percent of their actual size).

2. Making paper templates

Print each template on card-weight paper. Use scissors or a craft knife to cut out the envelope shape. Place the shape on a piece of decorative paper you want to make into an envelope and trace around it. Cut out the envelope, fold it and glue the edges using a glue stick. (In the case of the A7 and the Small Letter envelope, the outside edges of the outlines may be clipped off by your printer. You can deal with this either by estimating where the lines should be and cutting accordingly, or by tiling your print on more than one sheet and taping the pieces together before cutting.)

3. Using Photoshop

Open a scanned envelope template in Photoshop. Then open a photo or piece of scanned art or clip art and enlarge it to 8 1/2 inches by 11 inches or larger. Copy and paste the template into the art document, where it will appear in a separate layer. Use the marquee tool to select the dotted fold lines and then delete them. Print the image with the envelope outlines. Cut out the envelope, fold and glue.

More envelope ideas

A "LINED" ENVELOPE

You can create the look of a fine envelope lined with decorative paper by cropping an image to the outlines of an unfolded envelope and then printing, cutting and folding it.

DECORATED ENVELOPES

Both ready-made and handmade envelopes can be embellished using the same techniques used for greeting cards (see pages 82–85) using stickers, rubber stamps, glitter, doilies, buttons, metallic-ink pens, paper or cloth scraps, ribbon or stitching. If your decorated envelope will be sent in the mail, you may want to protect it (and the Post Office) by enclosing it in a larger kraft paper envelope.

Creating a lined envelope

I started by unfolding and scanning an A2 envelope (below) and brought the scan into Photoshop. Then I selected colorful buttons from my button jar and placed them good-side-down on my scanner to capture an image. I imported the button scan into the document containing the scanned envelope and then used the envelope image as a guide to trim away the button image (see above). I printed the trimmed image, cut out the envelope shape (using the actual unfolded envelope as a guide) and folded and glued my new envelope (left). You can also scan one of the templates on the opposite page and try decorating its inside surface with a scanned texture or photo.

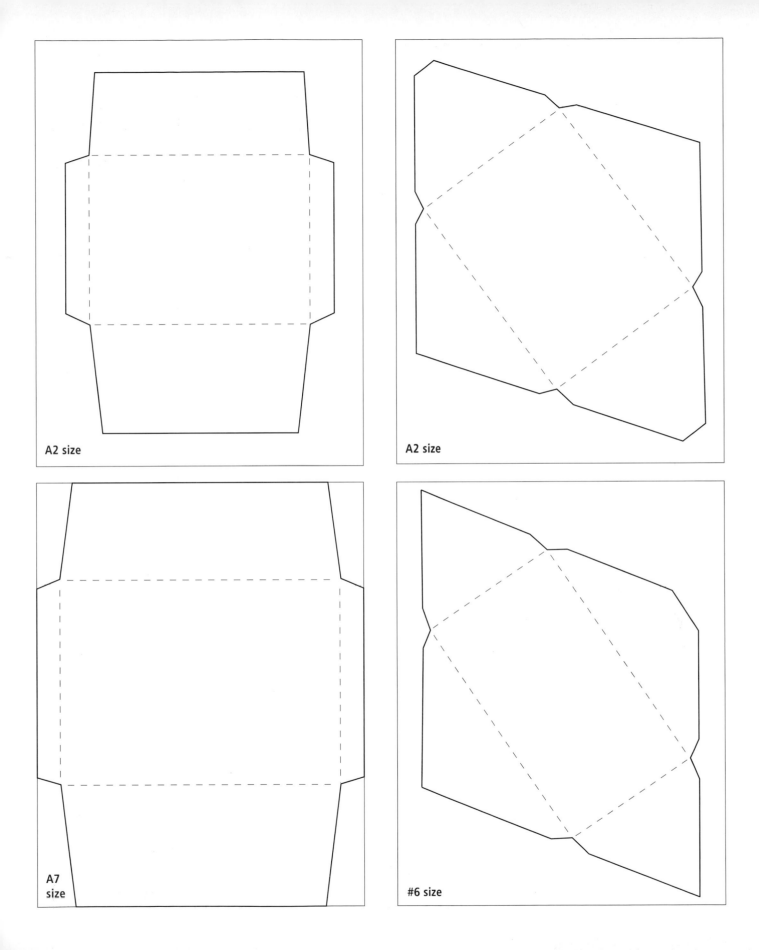

A2 size

A2 size

A7
size

#6 size

Creating Message Cards and Bookmarks

In addition to folded greeting cards, there are many ways to combine text and graphics to produce cards that inspire, remind, motivate or identify.

Cards with a message

I love collecting quotes. I also love finding good graphics and taking photographs. My computer makes it possible for me to combine these favorite words and pictures to create printed cards that are just right for me. Message cards can be made in many sizes and shapes—to be carried in a wallet, tucked into the edge of a mirror or slipped into a photo frame. Message cards can also be included in a letter or mailed as postcards.

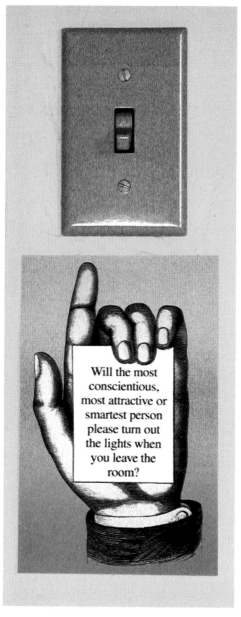

Gentle reminders

To encourage the members of my family to conserve electricity, I created these cards, based on an idea developed by Elizabeth W. Adler for a utility company. It's described in her book *Everyone's Guide to Successful Publications* (Peachpit Press, 1993). I scanned an old-fashioned pointing hand from *Handbook of Early Advertising Art* (Dover, 1956) and used Photoshop to remove the original text, add new text set in Times and add color gradients. I created two versions: one that points down to a light switch and one that points up, to accommodate the conditions in my home.

Slogans and affirmations

Twelve Step programs, beginning with Alcoholics Anonymous, have adopted various slogans to help their members remember key ideas. I used PageMaker to create a set of cards which include a slogan in large type and a related quote in smaller type, all in various weights of Garamond and Garamond Condensed. The type was placed over a lightly colored ornament, taken from *1500 Decorative Ornaments: CD-ROM and Book* (Dover, 2000). Cards such as these can be made in any size, to fit in a wallet, hang on a wall or place in a small frame on a desk. Easy Does It, Live and Let Live and Keep It Simple.

Theme and variations

Mahatma Gandhi, the great Indian spiritual and political leader, emphasized the importance of morality in public life, expounding his own version of the seven deadly sins. I scanned a fragment of Indian ornament from *Racinet's Historic Ornament in Full Color* (Dover Publication's 1988 reprint of the 1875 original) and used it in two ways: as a background for a card presenting the seven sins and as a border on a set of separate cards, each with a slight rewording of Gandhi's statements.

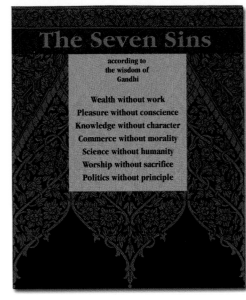

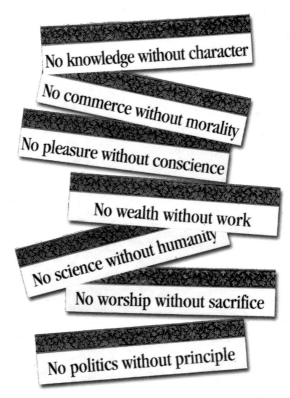

Do the right thing

The Gracious Queen—a figure who appeared to me in a dream—is a woman of mature wisdom who always says and does the right thing. When I am feeling annoyed, angry, tired or resentful and contemplating doing something negative, I sometimes think of her and ask myself: "What would the Gracious Queen do?" To remind myself to ask this question more often, I created a special card in the style of an old fruit crate label. I created the art in Illustrator, using the Friz Quadrata typeface and the gentle personage of Jadwiga of Anjou, queen of Poland in 1384, scanned from *Racinet's Full-Color Pictorial History of Western Costume* (Dover, 1987).

Words over images

"In wildness is the preservation of the world" is one of my favorite quotes from Henry David Thoreau. To remind myself of it, I scanned a photo of the beautiful redwoods in my backyard and used Photoshop to create a lightened panel at the bottom of the image, creating a suitable background for text. I then placed the image in PageMaker and set the type in Garamond Book Condensed. I created and printed the image at 5- by 7-inch size so that it would fit into a ready-made acrylic photo frame.

Bookmarks and bookplates

A bookplate pasted inside the front cover tells us that this book belongs to someone who loves to read. Try printing bookplates on self-adhesive label paper, either in color or black-and-white. A sheet of bookplates makes a nice gift for a reader. So does a set of decorative bookmarks, enhanced with inspiring quotes!

A book of her own

To create a bookplate for my daughter Molly I scanned a scrap of decorative paper and used Photoshop to change its hue from beige to pink. I then imported an illustration from *Books, Reading and Writing Illustrations: CD-ROM and Book* (Dover, 1998), positioned it over the scan and slightly lightened the area behind it. I imported the finished image into PageMaker, added a black border and set type in Goudy, using wide letterspacing and separating the lines with hairline rules. The design was printed on self-adhesive label paper and cut to size.

Marking my place

I've been making my way through Tolstoy's *War and Peace* and wanted a sturdy bookmark to keep my place. I found an expressive illustration of a woman reading in *Books, Reading and Writing Illustrations: CD-ROM and Book* (Dover, 1998). I combined it with a quote from *The Quotable Woman* by Elaine Partnow (Corwin Books, 1977), set in Guardi Roman. I printed the bookmark on a slightly flecked paper, cut it to size and pasted it onto a piece of blue decorative paper. I then used a self-adhesive laminating sheet to laminate and protect both sides of the bookmark. I punched a hole in the top and used beige flecked yarn and gold flecked pink embroidery thread to create a braided tassel. It could also have been laminated using a Xyron machine (see page 119).

Bookmarks with quotes

To promote *The Arts and Crafts Computer* I created a set of bookmarks that feature quotes on craft and creativity. I placed the quotes in narrow columns on a single page, over a light gray engraving of a hand. I printed the page on off-white textured paper and cut it into five separate bookmarks. The book title and my name and address are printed on the opposite side. The bookmarks can be reassembled to reveal the whole hand. Bookmarks from a puzzle-like set such as this one could be tucked into a letter and sent to a friend one at a time. To receive a copy of the set, send a self-addressed stamped envelope to me at the address listed at the end of this book.

Creating Artist Books

We all know what a book is, but what is an "artist book"? There are many conflicting definitions, especially in the book arts world, but one simple guideline is that an artist book combines *text* and *images* with a book *structure* that usually involves pages made of paper. Of course any one of these elements can be missing or altered: some artist books have no words at all, some have no pictures, and some have pages made of wood or metal, or no pages at all.

Until recently most artist books have been made using traditional art methods to produce the text and images, along with hand bookbinding techniques to create the structure. But more and more book artists are using the computer to help them in the creation of text and images, especially since a computer and printer make it so much easier to create the "multiples" required to create a limited edition of fifty to 100 books. Any of the digital image-making and typography techniques I've demonstrated so far can be used to create the images and text for an artist book. These can be made entirely within the computer or by combining computer art with traditional art. As to book structure, on the next eight pages I'll describe some of the most basic forms. There are many more complex and fascinating book structures to explore. You can learn more about this fascinating art by looking at some of the book arts resources listed at the end of the book.

Ways to Bind Book Pages

Most manufactured books, such as the one you're reading right now, are bound by creating a groups of "signatures" (groups of pages stitched into a pamphlet) which are glued to a hard or soft cover. However, there are many more simple ways of binding together pages for an artist book.

Stapling
A heavy-duty staple gun can be used to staple together a book that's not too thick.

Spiral binding and comb binding
Quick copy stores often offer binding services including spiral and comb bindings.

Wire-O
You can purchase machines for doing your own Wire-O type of spiral binding at home.

Punched holes
One or more holes can be punched in book pages, which are then bound using string, ribbon, raffia, cord, metal rings, braids, key chains or screw posts (also known as Chicago screws).

Sewing with zigzag stitch
Use your sewing machine and a wide zigzag stitch to sew down the edge of a group of pages.

Door hinges
Use a door hinge or cabinet hinge as a book structure. Glue paper to the outside of the hinge. Glue the ends of an accordion folded strip to the inside surfaces.

An artist's book
In her typography class at College of the Redwoods, my daughter Florence Ashford was asked to typeset a quote and present it in any printed form. She created a board book with pages made of Davey board covered with metallic and matte origami paper (see "Creating Hard Covers for an Accordion Book" on page 97). The boards are decorated with pasted collages made of nineteenth century clip art scanned from various Dover books, cut with scissors and combined with decorative paper. She printed sections of the quote onto pieces of transparency film, which alternate with the decorated pages. The book was bound with metal rings passed through punched holes.

The 3-Hole Pamphlet Stitch

Basic sewing instructions

1. Punch holes
Punch three evenly spaced holes through the fold of the booklet, from the inside to the outside, using a large sewing needle. Make sure all the sheets making up the booklet are evenly aligned. Secure them with paper clips if necessary.

2. Cut thread
Cut a piece of heavy, non-breakable thread to at least four times the height of your booklet and thread it on the same needle you used to make the holes.

3. Sew through center hole
Start on the inside of the booklet and pass the needle and thread through the center hole to the outside. Leave a few inches of thread hanging loose on the inside of the booklet.

4. Sew through second hole
Pass the needle and thread through either one of the remaining holes, back to the inside of the booklet.

5. Sew through third hole
Pull the thread all the way across the inside fold of the booklet to the third hole and pass the needle and thread through it back to the outside.

6. Sew through the center hole again
Pass the needle and thread through the center hole again, this time coming from the outside to the inside of the booklet.

7. Tie a knot and trim
Remove the needle from the thread. Make sure that the two loose ends of the thread lie on either side of the thread that stretches along the inside fold. Pull the ends of the thread snug and tie them in a knot or bow. Trim the ends.

Alternative decorative sewing
To create a decorative bow on the outside of the booklet, start your sewing from the outside of the booklet so that your loose ends of thread end up on the outside rather than the inside and can be tied into a decorative knot or bow. You can try using decorative embroidery threads. You can also try punching larger holes to accommodate heavier yarns or raffia.

Simple Book Structures

The most elementary book form is the *folio* (from the Latin word for "leaf"), which is a single sheet folded in half to create four "pages" that can be viewed in sequence. The folded sheet leads directly to two of the most popular handmade book forms: the stitched pamphlet and the accordion-fold book.

Stitched pamphlet books

A pamphlet consists of two or more folios stitched together through the fold to create a booklet. Pamphlets are traditionally bound with strong thread sewn through small holes that are punched through the fold with a needle or small awl.

Creating a fold-and-stitch photo book
To create an 8-page booklet, print images on both sides of a single sheet of paper and then fold it in half twice. Use a craft knife to trim the outside edges and sew the booklet through the center fold using a 3-hole pamphlet stitch. You can add type to the first page to create a cover. The booklets above were created by John Odam, to whom I am indebted for this idea. John is my co-author on *Start with a Scan* (Peachpit Press, 2000). He was born and raised in England and tells me that every English school child learns to do the pamphlet stitch.

Computer images and text can be added to a pamphlet book in two ways: either by printing directly on the pages, which are then folded and stitched. Or by cutting and pasting computer-printed elements onto blank pamphlet pages. The pamphlet method can also be used to create journal-type books that have blank pages but decorated covers.

FOLD-AND-STITCH PHOTO BOOK
A charming way to present photos is to print them on both sides of a single sheet of paper and then fold, trim and stitch the paper to create a small booklet. This simple book form provides a lovely way to preserve photo memories of a day in the country, a wedding, a holiday gathering or scenes of the seasons. If you have a digital camera, you'll be able to produce a photo booklet the same day you take the pictures. Be sure to use a heavier weight paper that's coated on both sides, so the printed images don't bleed through. Booklets can be made of a single sheet folded twice to create eight pages, or of two sheets folded and combined to create sixteen pages.

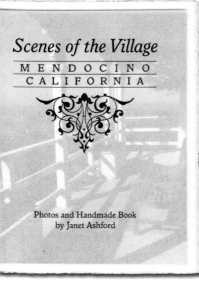

Scenes of the Village

M E N D O C I N O
C A L I F O R N I A

Photos and Handmade Book
by Janet Ashford

Positioning and printing

The diagrams at right show how to position the images so that each one is right side up after the paper is folded. Set up a document in Photoshop or in a page layout program, import your photo images, and arrange and rotate them as necessary. Create one document for each side of the paper. Crop each photo to 4-inch by 5-inch size so that each document contains an 8-inch by 10-inch block of images and can be printed on one side of a single letter-size sheet. Trim away the white margins after the printed paper is folded. I used Great White Imaging and Photo Paper, matte finish because it's heavy weight, coated on both sides, and acid-free.

Embellishing a fold-and-stitch booklet

To create an outer cover for my photo book I used a piece of watercolor paper with torn edges. To create a cover illustration I used Photoshop to set type on a digital photo and printed it, cut it and pasted it onto the cover. To add a fly leaf I used PageMaker to type the booklet title and printed it onto a piece of translucent vellum tracing paper. This was trimmed, folded and wrapped around the signature of printed photos (see above). The photos, vellum and cover were stitched through with thread, using the three-hole pamphlet stitch described on the opposite page. Fold-and-stitch books such as this one can be popped into an envelope and sent as a combination greeting card and gift.

5	4
8	1

3	9
2	7

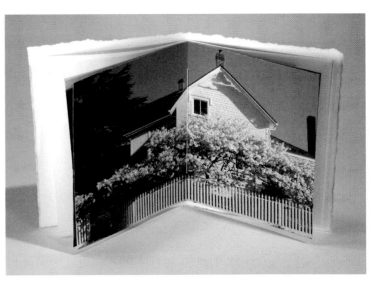

Creating a center spread

Notice that pages 4 and 5 will fall in the center of the booklet and can be used for one large photo if you like. Likewise, pages 1 and 8 (the front and back pages) can be used for a single photo spread.

Nobody made a greater mistake than he who did nothing because he could only do a little.

—Edmund Burke, quoted in *50 Simple Things You Can Do to Save the Earth* (The Earthworks Group, Earthworks Press, 1989)

Accordion-fold books

An accordion book is made of a single sheet of paper (usually long and narrow) that is folded in equal sections with the folds alternating between "valleys" and "mountains." The pages of an accordion book can be turned and read in sequence as with a pamphlet book, but they also can be spread out and viewed all at once. Just one side or both sides of an accordion book can be filled with text and images. When the book is closed the accordion pages collapse onto themselves. At its simplest the accordion structure requires no binding, for the "pages" are already connected. But hard covers can be added to the first and last pages of the accordion to provide protection and to help the book stand up on its own.

An action-oriented accordion book

At a local thrift shop I found a box of paper scraps, including some long narrow strips of colored paper. This inspired me to create an accordion book on the theme of recycling and other earth-friendly actions. I folded one strip of green paper to create an eight-panel accordion and decorated it with a combination of found paper and digital output. The found paper backgrounds were taken from Encore Exotica, a collection of interesting paper scraps (see Resources). I used PageMaker to create type for the book, using several different typefaces. I also took some digital camera shots of my garden, compost and recycling bins to create images for the front and back covers and the inside. The covers were made by gluing digital photo prints to pieces of book board, following the method described on the opposite page.

Creating Hard Covers for an Accordion Book

Books are traditionally bound with hard covers made by pasting paper or book cloth to pieces of stiff board. Books often have a cover made of a front, back and spine, but an accordion book does not require a spine. The covers for the books shown on pages 93 and 96 were made as described below. For complete instructions on making hard covers for accordion books, pamphlets and journals see *Cover to Cover* or *Making Books By Hand*, both listed in the Resources section.

Cutting book board

Book board (also called binder's board or Davey board) is an archival type of stiff cardboard used for book covers. It can be ordered from businesses that sell bookbinding supplies (see Resources). Book board is about $1/8$-inch thick and is best cut with a good quality paper cutter. But I've had success cutting it with a craft knife. With a fresh blade, cut carefully against a metal straight edge and stroke firmly, but not too hard, thirty or forty times to gradually cut down through the board.

Burnishing with a bone folder

A bone folder (shown on page 75) is an indispensable tool for bookbinding. After you've glued paper onto a surface, use the flat edge of the bone folder to burnish it down and stroke out any air bubbles. Use the pointed tip of the bone folder to make the small crease required in step 4 below.

1. Cut and glue the board and paper

Cut two pieces of board to the size you want, which should be just a tad larger than the finished size of your book. Cut two pieces of paper and make sure that they extend $1/2$ to 1 inch all around the board. Use PVA liquid glue and a flat stiff-bristle brush to spread an even layer of glue onto one side of each board and press each one down in the center of the wrong side of the paper.

2. Trim the corners

Using scissors or a craft knife, cut each corner of the paper at a 45 degree angle. Position the cuts so that each one is about as far away from the corner of the board as the board is thick.

3. Glue the top and bottom edges

Spread a thin, even coat of glue on the top and bottom flaps. Press them down onto the board and burnish them with a bone folder. Place a piece of waxed paper over each flap as you burnish, to protect other surfaces from seeping glue.

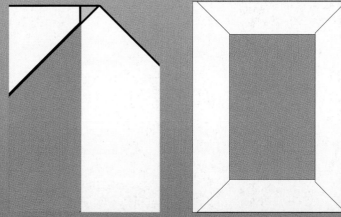 

4. Crease the corner edges

Use the pointed end of a bone folder to press down the excess paper in each corner of the top and bottom flaps, as shown in the diagram.

5. Glue the side edges

Apply glue to the side edges, fold them over and burnish them down. Place waxed paper over each cover and press them under heavy books for a few hours.

6. Attach the accordion

Apply glue to the back of the first page of your accordion book and burnish it down onto the inside of the front cover board. Then apply glue to the last page and burnish it onto the inside of the back cover board. Fold the entire book closed and press it under weights, using waxed paper to protect the glued surfaces from each other.

Combining pamphlets and accordions

Now that you know how to create pamphlets and accordion books, you can combine them to create more complex book structures. It's possible to sew pamphlets into the folds of accordion books and also to bind accordion pages into a pamphlet. These are just two of the many book structures that can be created by combining pamphlets, accordions and other forms. To learn more, consult some of the books listed in the "book arts" section in Resources. Among the most helpful are *Making Books By Hand*, *Cover to Cover* and *Non-Adhesive Binding: Books Without Paste or Glue*.

Drawing on the table
One of our favorite restaurants covers its tables with white paper and provides crayons for patrons to use while waiting for dinner. My daughter Florence and I drew the faces above (left column) and I scanned them to create art for a *dos à dos* book. Since the original drawings were too large to fit entirely on the scanner, I used only the center section of each and also created versions in which the colors are converted to their opposites (right column).

CREATING A DOS À DOS BOOK
The French term *dos à dos* refers to a seat or carriage in which the occupants sit back to back. It's also the name of a dance figure in which the partners circle around each other back to back

Creating the inner pamphlets
To create the two pamphlets for my dos à dos book I followed the same procedure as for the fold-and-stitch books described on pages 94-95, except that instead of placing a single image on each "page" I filled each side of the paper with one large image, putting a positive image on one side and its negative version on the other. When these were folded down and trimmed, different areas of the face images fell on different pages and some were upside down, creating a bizarre effect that fit the style of the drawings.

Binding back to back
To create the accordion structure I folded a piece of heavyweight purple paper into three equal sections, forming it into the shape of a letter "Z." I used thread to sew a pamphlet into each of the two folds, using the 3-hole pamphlet stitch described on page 94. I then printed four small face images and glued them onto the outer and inner covers of the accordion.

(in contra dancing and squares we often hear the caller sing out: "Allemande left, do-se-do, now swing your partner"). Dos à dos is also a book form in which two small pamphlets are sewn into a short accordion book, folded in a "Z" shape. The book can be opened from either end, with either cover functioning as the front.

ADDING AN ACCORDION TO A PAMPHLET

Binding accordion pages into a pamphlet has the effect of creating fold-outs, which in some artist books extend for many pages beyond the main body of the book. I created a simple version of this form using a single sheet of legal-size paper.

Creating the art work

I used PageMaker to lay out the book's images, importing them from *Books, Reading and Writing Illustrations: CD-ROM and Book* (Dover, 1998). In PageMaker I assigned a color to each image and converted each one to "black-and-white" rather than "grayscale" mode so that its white areas would be transparent. I layered each image over a rectangle filled with solid color and also placed a small circle in a contrasting color behind the head of each reader.

Laying out the pages

Using a piece of legal-size typing paper, I created a dummy marked with page numbers to guide me in placing the art work for my combination book. Pages 6 and 7 are the center spread of the inner pamphlet page, while pages 4, 9, 3 and 10 are part of a single accordion that can be unfolded to extend out from the main pamphlet. The dotted lines in the diagrams below indicate where the paper should be cut. Each diagram indicates one side of a single legal-size sheet of paper.

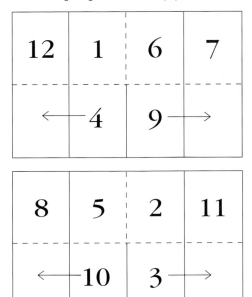

Assembling the book

I printed the PageMaker layouts on both sides of a single piece of good-quality, cream-colored book paper, which I had trimmed to 8 1/2-inch by 14-inch legal size from a larger sheet. The result looks remarkably like a silk-screened print. I used an X-Acto knife to cut the printed paper in half lengthwise. The lower strip containing pages 3, 4, 9 and 10 is the accordion section. I folded it to create four equal sections. The remaining strip was cut in half widthwise to create two pieces which I folded in half to create the two folios of a pamphlet. The pages were stitched together so that pages 1 and 12 (the front and back covers) were on the outside, the accordion page was next, and the remaining pamphlet page was in the center of the book.

Coloring Books

Many wonderful coloring books—with images of birds, butterflies, animals, historic costumes and designs from different cultures—are sold by Dover Publications. But you may want to create a unique coloring book for a special child or grown-up friend. One easy way to do this is to scan black-and-white line drawings from various sources (including Dover's books), print them on plain paper and bind the sheets together. You could print on legal-size sheets (8 1/2 by 14 inches) or letter-size sheets (8 1/2 by 11 inches), fold them in half and stitch them together using the 3-hole pamphlet stitch described on page 94. You can also bind the book by stitching the edges of the sheets with a simple Japanese stab binding, as I did here. To create a variety of backgrounds—and to honor future generations—I printed my coloring book on "tree-free" papers, including sheets made of recycled currency, old blue jeans, organic cotton, hemp, wheat straw, kenaf, coffee and bananas. For more information on paper see "The Politics of Paper" on page 69. For more ideas for children's gifts see pages 120-127.

Creating an initial coloring book

To create a coloring book for my five-year-old cousin Emily, I used initial E's from *Decorative Letters: CD-ROM and Book* (Dover, 1997), combined with adjectives starting with "e," culled from *Roget's Thesaurus*. In PageMaker I placed an initial and an adjective on each half of a letter-size page, arranging the artwork so that when each sheet was folded there would be an image on each side of the folded page. I left wide outer margins to leave room for the binding. I printed the book pages on a laser printer on seven kinds of "tree-free" paper and included a listing of them on the last page of the book. The papers include:

• Arboken's DP3 Agri-Pulp (wheat straw, post-consumer waste and chalk)

• Crane's Old Money (recycled currency), Denim Blues (old jeans), and Continuum Kenaf (kenaf and cotton)

• Costa Rica Natural's Banana and Coffee papers (post-consumer waste and agricultural by-products)

• Green Field Paper Company's Green Fields, Coyote Brown (hemp and organic cotton)

You can order a Treefree Sampler Pack from Green Earth Office Supply (see Resources).

I sewed the book with waxed black cord using a 7-hole stab binding (see opposite page) and added tassels of variegated yarn, with beads knotted onto the ends of the yarn and the cord.

A Simple Japanese Stab Binding

The pages for a book bound by the Japanese stab method are traditionally folded and stacked with the folded edge outward and the cut edges near the binding. This makes it possible to print the images for the book on one side of the sheet only, although more paper is used in the making of the book.

Getting ready

To prepare for a stab binding, fold all the book pages, line them up into a "book block" and clamp the pages together using paper clips or paper clamps. Then use a pencil and ruler to mark seven evenly spaced holes on the top page, near the cut edges of the book block.

Sewing instructions for a 7-hole stab binding

Use yarn, embroidery floss, heavy gauge waxed thread, linen or necklace cord threaded onto a needle. A blunt tapestry needle works best, but a regular large sewing needle will do. The following instructions are for creating a bow or tassels that will appear on the front of the book. The dotted lines indicate the thread that's at the back of the book.

Punching holes

Depending on the thickness of the book, you can then use a large sewing needle or an awl to stab through the pencil marks to create holes or "sewing stations." Since my book was fairly thick, I used a small nail and hammered it through each hole marker into a piece of wood placed under the book block, piercing the wood just slightly so I could pull the nail out again and go on to the next hole.

1. Cut a piece of thread at least four times the length of the edge of the book. Sew through the first hole at the top left of the book, from front to back, leaving a 3 to 4 inch tail.
2. Bring the thread around the top edge of the book and sew back down through the first hole, to the back of the book.
3. Bring the thread around the left edge of the book and sew back down through the first hole, to the back of the book.

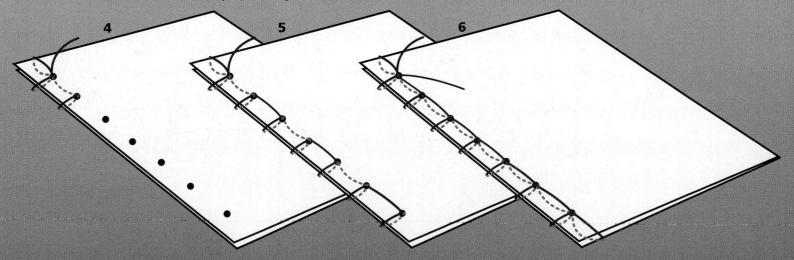

4. With your thread still at the back of the book, sew upward through the second hole, from back to front, sew around the left edge and through the second hole again, from back to front.
5. Your thread is now at the front of the book. Sew downward through the third hole, from front to back, and around the left edge and through the third hole again, from front to back. Continue alternating steps 4 and 5 until you reach the last hole. Your thread should be at the back of the book as you pass through the last hole.

6. Sew around the bottom edge of the book and back down through the last hole. Now make a running stitch back up to the first hole. To do this, sew upward through the sixth hole, downward through the fifth, upward through the fourth, downward through the third and upward through the second. Now, instead of going downward through the first hole, slip your needle and thread under the stitch that's around the left edge at the first hole and tie a knot with the loose thread that you left hanging there. Trim the threads, or tie them into a bow, or add beads to decorate them.

6 Crafting Gifts and Decorations

Capture it all

The weather was perfect when I visited Fort Ross, an old Russian settlement in Northern California. Pointing south with a digital camera, I took three photos of the shore near the fort, opened them in Photoshop and positioned them so that they overlap to create a whole image. I then added a drop shadow behind each one to make them look like photo prints lying on top of each other. I printed the image on glossy paper and trimmed and framed it to create an image that displays the scene and also subtly draws attention to the technology used to capture it.

OW DELIGHTFUL to turn a digital image of a flower or a face into a well-crafted object that I can hold in my hand, place on a shelf, use in my home, or wrap up to give as a gift. There are many ways to use photos and scanned art to create games, toys, home decor items, holiday ornaments, boxes and bags, party decorations and gift wrappings. Most of the projects in this chapter are made with paper but some are printed on special new media such as transparencies, magnet sheets, and cloth. For more information see "Going Beyond Paper" on page 111.

Showcasing Photos and Art

We all have photo albums or boxes full of 4 by 6 glossy prints. But treasured photos of places and people can be enjoyed in many other ways. First, edit your scanned photos to optimize color and contrast (refer to Chapter 2, Working with Photos and Scans, for tips on how to edit and enhance digital images). Then try some of the techniques shown here for turning your photos or other scanned art into gifts or playful objects.

Photo panoramas

Sometimes it takes more than one shot to really capture a beautiful scene. Standing in one spot, take several photos (with your digital or conventional camera), rotating a little to left or right with each shot. These photos can be assembled to create a wide panorama that does more justice to an impressive expanse of ocean, mountains or desert, a cityscape or even scenes of your own backyard.

Friends indeed
I used a digital camera to capture a quick series of shots of my daughter Molly and her friend Diana. In Photoshop I cropped each photo to a circle shape, then arranged them in a grid to print on a sheet of stickers, using a scan of the sticker template as a guide.

Photo stickers

Remember cramming into a booth with your friends to capture funny photos with your faces mushed together and tongues sticking out? Use a conventional or digital camera to take photos like these of your kids or friends, then edit and crop them to fit a sheet of stickers. Stickers make great gifts and can be attached to book covers, journals, scrapbook pages, lockers and bedroom walls.

Stand-up silhouettes

With your camera in hand, catch your friends or family doing something that tells a story about who they are—mowing the lawn, setting out to trick-or-treat or enjoying a hug. Stand back far enough to get their whole bodies in the shot. Then use Photoshop or a similar program to select and delete the background, leaving just the people surrounded by white. Print the images on glossy paper and mount them on foam core board, poster board or some other stiff paper, applying adhesive with photo mount, a Xyron machine, glue stick or PVA glue. Use a very sharp craft knife to carefully cut out the figures. If you have the patience, try cutting away all the white background. If not, just cut close to the edge of the figures, leaving an even thickness of white all around. Cut a vertical slot in the bottom and insert a small slotted stand, or slip the figures into a holder to make these little people stand up by themselves on a shelf, a window sill or mantel.

A Scot's a Scot for all that
My friend Hugh is a Scotsman through and through, with or without a kilt. My photo of him playing the highland pipes at music camp is a perfect subject for a stand-up silhouette. I used Photoshop to delete the background around him, printed the silhouette on photo glossy paper, glued it to poster board, then cut around it with a craft knife.

Stickers of all kinds
Sticker sheets are available with both round and rectangular sticker shapes in many sizes. I used Avery's Big Round Stickers, which were part of a packet of removable stickers that can be removed without leaving a residue and reapplied to another surface. The pack comes with a template and instructions for laying out images in several different programs. Sticker sheets are also available on photo quality glossy paper.

Mouse pads

There are at least three kinds of mouse pads that can be embellished with computer printed photos or art: photo frame, iron-on transfer, and printable.

PHOTO FRAME MOUSE PADS

Camera and craft stores sell mouse pads with a window into which you can slip a 4-inch by 6-inch photo. These kits can be used with conventionally printed photos or with photos you print yourself.

IRON-ON TRANSFER MOUSE PADS

Invent-It and Micro Format both make a blank mouse pad that can be decorated with iron-on transfer paper.

PRINTABLE MOUSE PADS

Create-A-Pad produces a mouse pad with a canvaslike surface and nonslip backing that's thin enough to be printed directly through an inkjet printer. The 7-inch by 9 $1/2$-inch pad punches out of a letter-size sheet, so you can bleed your image off the edge of the pad.

Coasters

Micro Format makes 3 $1/2$-inch blank coasters from the same thick material used for their mouse pads. The coasters can be decorated using iron-on transfer paper, which is included in the coaster kit. Thinner coasters could be made by printing a group of images directly onto a Create-A-Pad mouse pad and then cutting them apart.

Printing a mouse pad
When I lived near Cardiff Beach north of San Diego, I photographed some of the many spontaneous rock sculptures that were created there for months by an unknown artist. I kept a print in my photo frame mouse pad to remind me of the value of balance. The surface of my mouse pad finally wore out and I recently used the same image to create an inkjet printed mouse pad, using Create-a-Pad. (The company notes that the $1/32$-inch thickness of their pad may produce less wrist pain than thicker pads.)

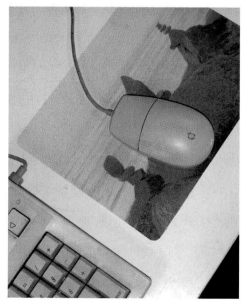

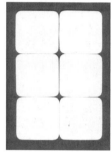

Creating coasters
I used Micro Format's EZ Transfer Coaster Kit to make a set of six coasters (ten coasters are included in the kit), using art from *500 Full-Color Decorative Illustrations: CD-ROM and Book* (Dover, 2000). To create a template for placement and size, I put six coasters on my scanner and scanned them into Photoshop. I copied and pasted in six art images and positioned them over circle backgrounds that I created in Photoshop. I printed the color image on the iron-on transfer paper included in the kit, cut each coaster image apart and ironed them onto the coasters.

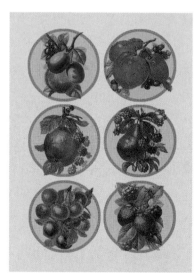

Canvas and watercolor paper

When a photo is altered using a digital filter (see page 39) it can look more like a drawing or painting—and when a filtered image is printed on textured paper it can look a lot like hand-painted art. I applied a dry brush filter to a photo of tulips and used it to test several kinds of specially coated, textured inkjet papers. The coatings, applied to textured paper or canvas, are designed to help retain image sharpness. (Sometimes when images are printed on uncoated textured paper they lose focus due to ink spreading or "dot gain.") Surprisingly, my favorite turned out to be traditional, uncoated Strathmore watercolor paper.

Rich and soft versus crisp and clear
Strathmore artist's watercolor paper provided rich color and good contrast for my filtered photo. The slight spreading of the ink as it is absorbed by this uncoated paper adds a softness that gives richness to the image. For printing an unfiltered photo, in which accuracy of detail is more important, a coated paper designed for digital printing (such as Artist Watercolor Paper from Mirage Inkjet Technology) may be a better choice.

Making a photo more "painterly"
I took this photo of tulips in bloom in Tennessee in April, using a conventional 35 mm camera. I scanned a 4-inch by 6-inch print and cropped the image to focus on the flowers and also to eliminate the red tulips at the right, which were so richly colored they oversaturated the film. I applied the Dry Brush filter in Photoshop to soften the photo and create a painterly effect.

Almost handmade
I left wide margins around my tulip image and framed the Strathmore paper print in a pre-cut double mat and simple wooden frame. The print does not look like a real painting, but it does look softer and less hard-edged than much computer art.

Paper picture frames

Decorative paper makes a pretty frame for a small photo or print. Small mats (7 by 9 inches or smaller) can be covered with computer printed images such as a photo or a scanned copy of a special paper that you don't want to cut. Printed text or sheet music also make interesting textural frames. Glue the digital print to a mat that already has an opening in it, then carefully cut an "X" shape through the center of the print, fold the edges back and glue them to the back of the mat. Or even easier, print your design on a piece of heavyweight paper and use a craft knife to cut out an opening. A paper frame works especially well for framing photos or art that will be slipped into a small acrylic desk frame.

Restoring and framing an old print

A girl admiring the first robin of spring is the topic of a sentimental print that my father kept in a small wooden frame. Over the years the print became brittle, cracked and torn. I removed it from the frame, scanned it, cropped away the torn edges and increased the color saturation. I reduced the size of the image and printed it on glossy paper. Then, to create a decorative paper frame, I used PageMaker to type Gerard Manley Hopkins' poem "Nothing is so beautiful as spring," using a typeface called Monet Impressionist from the P22 Type Foundry. This font, created in conjunction with the Albright-Knox Art Gallery in Buffalo, New York is based on the French artist Claude Monet's handwriting and is described as "a semi-legible script font intended for decorative, rather than communicative purposes." I printed the text in light brown on a piece of cream-colored flecked paper, cut a rectangular hole in the middle and inserted the print and paper mat back into the original wooden frame.

Using Plastic Craft Kits

Clock kits

At least two companies make ready-made plastic wall clocks that can be decorated by inserting a printed sheet. Create-A-Clock kit (available from Flax Art & Design and Micro Format) has a rectangular acrylic frame that holds an 8-inch by 10-inch image. The Dec-O-Clock™ kit (from Nasco Arts & Crafts) is round with a white plastic frame and takes art that's trimmed to an 8 ¹/₂-inch diameter circle. Nasco also sells battery-powered clock movements, metal numerals and wooden clock bases for making your own decorative clocks.

Snap-together kits

Several companies sell plastic items that can be decorated by inserting photos or artwork that are printed from a computer. These include rulers, pencil cups, mouse pads and plant pots (from Nasco Arts & Crafts); drinking mugs, photo banks, trivets and toothbrush holders (from Micro Format); and snow globes and key chains (from both Nasco and Micro Format). The items can be used for home decorating or as gifts.

Decorating mugs

To create artwork for a snap-together drinking mug from Micro Format, I first measured the inside of the clear outer part and found I would need strips of artwork 10 inches long and 3 ³/₄ inches high. I scanned an ethnic cloth napkin at larger than actual size (to provide a little contrast with the napkin) and selected two areas at the dimensions I needed. Then I printed the art on photo glossy paper, cut out the strips and glued the ends together to create two paper columns. I inserted each one into a clear mug and snapped the white inner piece into place.

Creating a clock face design

A round clock kit, such as the Dec-O-Clock™ that I used, could be decorated with a photo of people or a landscape. But I couldn't resist creating a geometrical design that took advantage of the round space. I scanned the embroidered pocket of a vest from India, then copied and rotated parts of it to create a round design in Photoshop. I kept the densely patterned part of the design fairly small and added areas of plain solid color around it so that the hour, minute and second hands would be more visible. I added numerals in Palatino, printed the design on matte finish photo paper, and inserted it into the clock. I hung the clock on the wall in my office, where it complements the colors and patterns of some Thai embroideries hanging below it.

Exploring Special Media

The popularity of color inkjet printers has boosted the development of a variety of new printing media that cater to the home user. (For more details see "Going Beyond Paper" on page 111.) The intended use of each material is usually conveyed by the name; such as bumper sticker paper and window decal paper. But some materials, such as metallic papers or magnetic sheets, can be used in many ways and it's a good exercise in creative thinking to invent at least one extra way in which each material could be used.

Metallic paper

Metallic papers are available in shiny and matte surfaces, in gold, silver, bronze and pearlized tones, for both inkjet and laser printers. For examples of metallic paper projects see the altar box on page 115 and the angel ornament on page 131.

Bumper sticker paper

Bumper sticker paper is made of coated vinyl that's waterproof to stand up to car washes and rain. But in addition to car bumpers, it could also be used to decorate other items that get wet, such as birdhouses, sheds, lawn furniture, garden plant identification tags, or signs (such as a tag that adds "please" to a hardware store "no trespassing" sign).

Transparent and translucent media

WINDOW DECALS

Window decal material is a coated clear plastic that lets you print color images, then adhere them to glass. It's especially suited to printing stained glass designs and holiday decorations, as

Propaganda has a bad name, but its root meaning is simply to disseminate through a medium, and all writing therefore is propaganda for something. It's a seeding of the self in the consciousness of others.

—Elizabeth Drew, English/American writer and literary critic (1887–1965)

Expressing your views
The rear bumper of my car has become a billboard for a variety of political sentiments. Most of my bumperstickers were purchased, but I love being able to invent my own and print them on my inkjet printer. That way I can say exactly what I want, as long as it doesn't exceed about a dozen well-chosen words. I created my "born at home" bumpersticker art in Illustrator because that program has good tools for creating and manipulating type and color. I printed the art on IBM's Ink Jet Bumper Stickers paper to let people know that my children were indeed born at home. (If you'd like to know why, check the childbirth section of my web site at www.jashford.com).

Making and testing a window decal

To create a decal with the look of stained glass I scanned a round design from *Islamic Designs* (Stemmer House, 1995) and filled parts of it with black to create a heavy line design. I then filled the remaining white space with the light colors I wanted and started testing the print on Xerox window decal paper. I found that I needed to darken the colors quite a lot on screen (bottom) to produce a decal that looked like my initial color choices when it was adhered to a window and had light shining through it.

well as posting store hours, directions, or safety instructions. It can be removed from glass and reapplied, without leaving a residue.

WATER SLIP DECALS

Water slip decals can be applied to any smooth surface, such as glass, plastic or metal. They're often used to apply graphics to model cars but can also be used to adorn fingernails.

TRANSPARENCY AND "BACK LIT" FILM

Clear transparency film is used to create art for overhead projectors. It can also be used to create overlay pages (see page 93) and can be folded to make transparent bags and boxes (see page 129). Back lit film is used for art that will be lighted from behind, as with a store or trade show display. It can also be used to make small lamp or candle shades (see page 130).

SEE-THRU WINDOW POSTER

This one way product can be seen from the outside of a window but not from the inside. It can be used to make one-way signs for store windows and car windows and also funny one-way goggles and masks.

TRANSLUCENT VELLUM

Translucent vellum paper and envelopes can be used in a variety of projects, including book arts. I used a vellum flyleaf in my Fold-and-Stitch photo booklet, shown on pages 94–95.

Magnetic media

Many companies now make sheets of inkjet magnetic material that can be printed in color or black-and-white, left whole or cut into smaller pieces and used to make refrigerator magnets, word games, phone lists, business promotions, reminder signs, car signs, puzzles and picture frames. What fun! Any sort of photo, art, pattern or message can be printed on a magnet sheet and stuck to anything made of metal: appliances, file cabinets, metal furniture, tin cans and boxes. The Xyron 510 can also apply magnet material to paper or cloth (see page 119). The magnets shown here feature old fruit crate art and a favorite cartoon. See page 123 for a magnetic puzzle.

Preserving a cartoon

We often clip cartoons from the paper and stick them on the refrigerator. One of my favorites came from the San Diego *Reader* and was getting ragged. So I scanned it, cleaned up the scan and then decided to add color. I printed it on a magnet sheet and then slapped it onto the tin can in which I keep my rulers and templates. The alien is saying to the earthling, "On our planet we just reproduce and die, what do you do?" Scanning copyrighted material is okay for personal use, but permission is required if you want to reproduce it in a book or product. Cartoonist Pete Mueller was kind enough to grant me permission to reprint his cartoon in this book. It's copyright © 2000 by P. S. Mueller.

Making good use of a magnet sheet

One of my favorite Dover books is now on CD-ROM: *Full-Color Fruit Crate Labels* (Dover, 2000). I chose seven of my favorites, scaled them to the same width and arranged them to fit on a single letter-size magnet sheet. I printed a copy on paper first, to make sure nothing was clipped off. Then, after printing on the magnet sheet, I used a craft knife to cut the images apart. I was intrigued to see "Chief Seattle" brand apples from Washington, named after the famous Chief whose name was given to the city. I found a copy of his 1854 speech, typed up and printed the last section and secured it to my refrigerator using the magnets. "The white man will never be alone. Let him be just and deal kindly with my people, for the dead are not powerless."

Going Beyond Paper

There are now many kinds of printing "media" available for desktop printers, taking crafters beyond the limitations of conventional paper. Most of these new products are suitable only for inkjet printers (since laser printers use a dry toner that does not always adhere to non-paper surfaces) but some can be used with laser printers. Be sure to check the label to see what kind of printer can be used. Many of these special media can be purchased at stationery and office-supply stores and many can be ordered over the Internet. Contact information for all the manufacturers mentioned on this page is provided in the Resources section at the back of this book. When working with special or expensive media, be sure to print a test of your image on plain paper first, to check for placement, color and so on. Look for projects created with these special media throughout this chapter.

Magnetic media

Inkjet magnet sheets
- From Mirage, RoyalBrites, Invent-it and Canon
- Use for business cards, refrigerator magnets, photo frames, car signs, puzzles

Printing for cloth

Iron-on transfer papers
- From Mirage, Xerox, IBM, Invent-It, Epson, RoyalBrites and Canon
- Use to apply graphics to T-shirts, sweatshirts, fabric, tote bags, hats, aprons, quilt material
- Invent-It makes a dark fabric iron-on transfer for use with dark or brightly colored fabrics

Fabric carriers
- From Micro Format
- Use to guide any cotton or cotton/polyester fabric through your printer

Fabric sheets
- From Canon
- Sheets of printable fabric; designed for Canon's bubble jet printers, can also be used with inkjet printers
- Use to make pot holders and oven mitts, small purses, pillow covers, small stuffed animals and dolls

Bumperstickers
- From IBM and Invent-it
- Coated vinyl; use for bumperstickers and anything else (garden signs, birdhouse decorations) that will be used outdoors

Self-adhesive papers

Sticker paper
- From Avery, Invent-it, Epson
- Sticker paper is available in matte and glossy surfaces, both permanent and removable, in many sizes and shapes including round, rectangular and full-sheet
- Use to make party favors (put on paper cups), decorate school notebooks, seal envelopes, create ID tags for belongings, make student or employee awards, room decorations

Polysilk adhesive
- From Mirage
- A high quality, glossy, silky card weight sticker paper; use to cover special albums such as wedding or baby books

Clear adhesive labels
- From Avery, available for laser or inkjet in several sizes
- Use to create transparent labels for paper, wood, metal, glass items

Self-adhesive labels
- From Avery
- Use to create labels for presents, gift bags, storage boxes, folders, plastic and paper cups

Mouse pads

Iron-on transfer mouse pads
- From Invent-It and Micro Format

Printable mouse pads
- From Create-a-Pad
- Use to create personalized mouse pads

Coasters
- From Micro Format
- Apply iron-on transfer images to square coasters for hot and cold drinks.

Transparent and translucent media

Window decals
- From Mirage, Xerox, Invent-it and Jobo
- Use for window or mirror decorations; removable, can be applied to any smooth surface such as glass or metal; use to make holiday decorations, small shapes for lamps or candles; simulate stained glass designs

SuperCal decals
- From Micro Format
- This unique product creates "water slip" decals that can be applied to any smooth surface including glass, plastic, or fingernails. It's available with both clear and white backing

Transparency film
- From Mirage, IBM, Epson, Jobo and Canon
- Use to create art for overhead projectors; also can be used to make transparent folded boxes and other objects

Back lit film
- From Canon and Micro Format
- Use for art that will be lit from behind, as with a trade show display; can also be used to create lamp shades

"See-Thru Window Poster"
- From Micro Format
- Images printed on this one way product can be seen from the outside of a window but not from the inside. It can be used to make one-way signs for car or store windows

Translucent vellum
- From RoyalBrites
- Can be ordered from Paper Direct and Paper Access
- Use in a variety of projects requiring a paper that's semitransparent including overlay pages for book arts

Banner paper
- From Mirage, Invent-It, Epson
- Use for banners, larger size gift wrap, posters, decorative wall hangings

Puzzle kits

Printable puzzles
- Puzzle Clonzz from Compoz-A-Puzzle

Iron-on transfer puzzles
- From Compoz-A-Puzzle, Micro Format and Invent-It
- Use as greeting cards, party invitations or games

Canvas and watercolor paper

Artist canvas
- From Mirage, IBM, RoyalBrites, Jobo and Canon
- Use to give canvas texture to printed photos and art

Artist watercolor paper
- From Mirage
- Coated with a calculated dot gain to simulate an original watercolor

Metallic papers
Available in shiny and matte surfaces; laser printable metallic papers can also be ordered from Paper Access and Paper Direct

Silver reflective paper
- From Mirage
- Use to create Christmas cards, invitations and special portraits

Gold, silver and pearlized paper
- From Micro format
- Use to make rich-looking gift bags and boxes, holiday cards and ornaments.

More special media

3-D paper
- From Micro Format; includes 3-D glasses for viewing images

Body sticker tattoos
- From Invent-It and Beldecal

Fuzzy paper
- From Micro Format

Glow-in-the-Dark paper
- From Micro Format

Shrink plastic
- From Micro Format

Working with Cloth

Digital images can be applied to cloth in three ways: by using iron-transfer papers, by printing on specially prepared fabric sheets, or by using a fabric carrier.

Iron-on transfer papers

This special paper, sold by many companies, receives the ink from your printer as you print an image, then transfers the ink to fabric or other porous materials when you iron it down with a hot iron. Because you'll place your print face down on the cloth, be sure to print a mirror image of your art. (Use your imaging software to flip the image or else specify mirror image with your printer software.) Iron-on transfers can be used to apply art to ready-made items such as T-shirts, sweatshirts, tote bags, canvas lunch bags, hats and aprons, as well as to plain cloth that you can then include in a quilt, pillow or other sewing project. You'll get the best results when transferring images to white or light colored cloth. But some companies also sell special transfer papers for use with dark fabrics

What a strange machine man is! You fill him with bread, wine, fish, and radishes, and out comes sighs, laughter, and dreams.

—Nikos Kazantzakis, Greek novelist (1885–1957)

Decorating a tote bag

Nasco Arts & Crafts sells blank canvas tote bags that are large, sturdy and inexpensive. They're designed for decorating either by hand with fabric paints or with iron-on transfers. To decorate mine I scanned two antique Tarot cards from a French deck produced around 1750. I chose The Sun and The Moon, since these celestial entities are so intimately connected with the growing of the farmer's market produce I plan to carry in my bag. I scanned the two small cards at an enlarged size to fit the height of the bag and printed a reverse image of each one on a single sheet of transfer paper. I found that the rough woodcut style of the artwork fit nicely with the coarse texture of the canvas fabric. I am especially fond of playing card designs and find they make interesting images for computer art projects. For a list of other image ideas see "Images from Everywhere" on page 133.

Fabric carrier

One problem with printing cloth directly is that it's usually not stiff enough to feed through a printer without jamming. Micro Format solves this problem by selling a carrier that guides any cotton or cotton/polyester fabric through your inkjet printer.

Fabric sheets

Canon sells computer-printable fabric sheets which consist of white, 100 percent cotton cloth attached to a plastic backing that keeps it stiff. The sheets are A4 size (9 ¹/₂ by 14 inches) and are designed for use with Canon's bubble jet printers. But I was able to use the sheets successfully in my Epson inkjet printer.

Adapting art work for cloth

Direct Imagination provides several great nineteenth century graphic works on CD-ROM including *Costumes of China and Japan*, taken from Racinet's *Le Costume Historique*. Most of the art is provided in TIFF format but some of the designs have been converted to EPS format. I wanted to use a striking Chinese design with diagonal lines and wavelike forms, but I felt the solid black background would not look rich and dark enough when printed on absorbent cloth. So I opened the EPS art in Illustrator and changed the background color from black to red. I also copied some of the diagonal lines into the blank space at the top of the design, moved the cloud shapes down, and changed the proportions to make the art closer to the proportions of the fabric sheet.

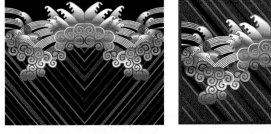

Sewing, Stitching, Quilting

Cloth that has been printed with photos or other artwork (either by iron-transfer or direct printing) can be incorporated into many sewing projects, sometimes combined with other cloth, plus trims and quilting stitches. Projects include:
- aprons
- bags with string closings (for jacks, marbles and other small treasures)
- cross stitch designs
- gift bags
- Christmas stockings
- dolls and doll clothes
- hand puppets
- oven mitts
- pillow covers
- pockets for jumpers and dresses
- pot holders
- purses
- quilts
- stuffed animals
- tea cozies
- tote bags
- wall hangings

Creating a fabric bag

After altering the Chinese design in Illustrator, I opened the file in Photoshop and printed it onto two fabric sheets from Canon. After letting them dry I sewed the two sheets together to create a bag that's about 7 by 9 inches. I sewed channels at the top of the bag, through which I threaded braided yarn that's used to close the bag.

Decorating Everyday Objects

Paper printed with digital images can be used to decorate many kinds of everyday household objects. Objects to decorate can be purchased new, gathered from around the house, or bought from garage sales and thrift stores. Images can be printed on sticker paper or on plain paper that you then glue on. Traditional decoupage techniques of cutting, gluing and varnishing can all be used with printed digital images.

Ready-made boxes

Art supply and craft stores sell small boxes in various shapes made of light wood, wood strips, binder's board, heavy paper and paper maché. Shapes include stars, hearts, circles, ovals, triangles, squares and rectangles. Some have lids, some with hinges. All can be decorated with computer printed paper. Some boxes come in nesting sets that are sized to fit inside each other. You can also buy flat, foldable boxes from office supply stores, drug stores or the Post Office.

Applying the art

First I applied a thin coating of silver paint to the box and lid. Then I printed the art for the lid and side strips on pieces of full sheet sticker paper. I used a craft knife to cut the side strips apart and carefully applied them to the box. I used scissors to cut out the oval lid decoration and carefully applied it. I then added a gold medallion sticker cut into four segments and press-on star stickers and gave the finished box a light coating of varnish.

Decorating an oval box

I bought a set of wooden nesting boxes from Nasco Arts & Crafts and decorated the largest one to hold my collection of foreign currency. To make a decorative strip around the box I first measured the distance from the box base to the bottom edge of the box lid, since I didn't want the lid to scrape whatever paper I glued onto the box. Then I scanned a number of bills, sized them all to the desired height, and packed them together into one Photoshop file, to make the best use of printing on a sticker sheet. The money included lire, Swiss francs and Canadian dollars from my own trips, as well as pretty examples from the Foreign Currency set sold by Fascinating Folds (see Resources). To create art for the box top I scanned a close-up of one bill and used Photoshop to paste it into a scan of the box lid itself, which I used as a guide for sizing and positioning the currency art. I then used the oval marquee to draw an oval that I could use to crop the art.

Scanned paper currency can also be used to make attractive wrapping paper. Make it yourself for smaller gifts. For larger gifts, try the oversized foreign currency sold by Flax Art and Design. Remember that it's illegal to reproduce currency at its actual size.

Creating a meditation box

I transformed a prosaic cigar box into a traveling meditation box, which can transform a corner of a hotel room into a small altar space. To create the cover art I scanned a line drawing from a book on Tantra yoga, autotraced it with Streamline and used Illustrator to add solid colors and gradients. I left some of the white spaces unfilled so that the metallic sheen would show through when I printed the design on silver and gold paper from Micro Format. To create art for the sides of the box I scanned an Indian ornament and also printed it on metallic paper. I took advantage of the blue paper with gold trim that was already on the cigar box by sizing my art to fit within its borders. I glued the printed art to the box using a light coat of PVA glue and then filled the box with items suitable for a traveling altar: a candle and holder, incense and holders, matches and two folding Thanka cards (from www.dharmapublishing.com).

"Found" boxes

Decorating gives new life to used containers such as the packing boxes that come in the mail, the wooden boxes in which perfumes and teas are sometimes sold and old cigar boxes. Cigar boxes can be decorated with any sort of art, including nineteenth century cigar box art (see *Old-Time Cigar Labels in Full Color* from Dover, 1996).

CIGAR BOXES

When I was a child I kept a cigar box in my desk at school. I used pieces of cardboard to divide it into compartments for my lunch money, my pencils and my prized hopscotch lager. What a treasure that box was to me! Cigar boxes are made of binder's board covered with paper and are constructed in much the same way as book covers. Instructions for making covered board boxes are found in *Making Memory Boxes* (see Resources). Cigar boxes can be used to store special things and also to create "theme boxes" of related small items with matching decorations.

Creating Theme Boxes

When we got married at the Court House in Kane County, Illinois, my former husband and I received a gift from the county along with our license. It was a small cardboard box containing items apparently essential for a new couple: gift certificates to local stores, mouthwash, and aspirin! Similar theme boxes (but hopefully containing more well-chosen items) can be created and decorated as gifts for holidays and special occasions.

Anniversary

Theater tickets, certificate for a massage (from you or from a masseuse), appointment card for dinner for two

Baby shower

Diaper pins, small book of baby names, certificate for free baby-sitting

Birthday

Gift certificate to a local book or music store, candy, dried flowers

Graduation or college survival

Phone card, money, postcards, stamps

Honeymoon or romance

"Do Not Disturb" door hanger, small bottle of wine or liqueur, candle and matches, incense, massage oil

Valentine's Day

Valentine card, chocolates, small pamphlet book of love poems

CRAFT TIP
To smooth air bubbles and remove excess glue when gluing prints to a surface, place a piece of waxed paper over the print and gently use the long straight edge of a bone folder to stroke outward in all directions from the center.

Tin cans and containers

I sometimes choose a brand of olive oil based on my desire to have the beautiful decorated can in which it's packed (see my painting on page 62). But the many less decorative tin cans and containers that come into our homes can be transformed with computer-generated art and used as pencil or brush holders, letter boxes, storage containers and so on. Thrift stores are a good source for tin boxes with lids, of the type used for holiday cookies and candies.

New Gifts from Old Junk

Check thrift stores and garage sales for used items that can be decorated with computer output. Just about anything made of wood, plastic or metal will work, including:

- candlesticks
- flower vases
- lamp bases and shades
- light switch plates
- lunch boxes
- mason jars
- metal and wooden trays and plates
- napkin rings
- picture frames
- plastic storage bins
- tissue box covers
- suitcases

Creating circular art

A friend gave me an old lidded can printed with a pretty black and gold design on its bottom part. But the lid was chipped so I painted it green and then searched through *1500 Decorative Ornaments CD-ROM and Book* (Dover, 2000) until I found an ornament that matched the design on the bottom of the can. I autotraced the TIFF ornament in Streamline, opened it in Illustrator and rotated copies around a central point in 40 degree increments to create a circular design. I gave the ornaments a gold fill and black stroke and then placed a radial gradient in a circle behind them. I printed the design on glossy photo paper, cut it out with scissors and glued it down with PVA. The tin now makes a good-looking holder for homemade cookies, candies or other treats.

Coloring black and white art

I like Altoids peppermints and consequently have a collection of empty tins which seem too cute and potentially useful to throw away. To decorate a batch of them I masked off the lids with masking tape and painted the bottoms green. While these were drying I scanned another tin by placing it directly on the scanner and in Photoshop removed all but the borders to create a template. Then, still working in Photoshop, I imported square and round ornaments from *Celtic Designs CD-ROM and Book* (Dover, 1997) and used the template as a guide for sizing and positioning them. I also cut one design in half and rotated it to create an ornament for the outside edges of the lid design. I lined up four lid designs in a grid and then added colors to the white spaces in the designs. I printed the designs on glossy photo sticker paper, cut them out with scissors and applied them to the box lids, where they fit snugly inside the red and gold border already printed there. These handsome little boxes with their hinged lids can be carried in a pocket or purse and make handy containers for guitar picks, matches, vitamins, and other small odds and ends.

Glass jars

I save empty food jars and use them for storing various things—nails, screws, buttons, dried beans—that are conveniently visible through the glass. In these cases the contents provide their own label and "decoration." But I also like to create decorative labels to identify contents that are more mysterious, for example a homemade salad dressing (when did I make it? does it have garlic?). Labels help me distinguish curry powder from tumeric, or green tea from black, making it easier to take advantage of buying such items in bulk, reducing the need for packaging. Labels also mark the date and contents of home canned fruits and vegetables and can transform a bottle of homemade herbal vinegar into a gift. Glass jars and bottles can be labeled using sticker paper (including the removable kind) and also with window cling decals (see page 109). Using cling decals makes it possible to easily change the label when the contents of the jar change. (Out-of-service decals can be stored between pieces of waxed paper until they're needed.)

Labels for bottles and jars

To transform an empty wine bottle into a decorative vessel for herb vinegar and to decorate a jar for a gift of Soup Bean Medley, I created labels using two pieces of art scanned from *The Art Nouveau Style Book of Alphonse Mucha* (Dover, 1980). (Read about Mucha's use of photography on page 30.) I printed the labels on self-adhesive glossy photo paper, cut them out with a craft knife and pressed them on. I sealed the vinegar bottle with a cork salvaged from another bottle and closed the bean jar with a lid sold by The Vermont Country Store (vermontcountrystore. com), which specializes in hard-to-find household items. The white vinyl lids fit large and small mouth canning jars, making it possible to easily reuse these jars for storage.

Editing art for labels

I used Photoshop to edit the color of the Mucha art, adding reds and yellows to warm up the palette. Then I deleted the type that Mucha had drawn to advertise a brand of liqueur and typed in my own text using a similar Art Nouveau-era font called Childs. To create the bean label I increased the contrast and color saturation of the scan, then sampled a pink color from the blossoms and used it to create a background for the type, which I filled with a red color and a green color also sampled from the art. To make the type stand out I added a stroke of black around it. The type was set in Ambrosia. Both fonts are from *24 Art Nouveau Display Fonts: CD-ROM and Book* (Dover, 1999).

Using Clear Labels

The boxes, cans, jars and bottles on the preceding four pages were decorated with opaque labels, sometimes in order to cover up an unsightly surface. But with brand new toys or boxes made of wood or painted metal, it's often attractive to let the underlying surface show through. Both clear labels and decals can be used to add graphics, text and splashes of color to objects such as the keepsake chest and metal case shown here. A variety of similar unfinished and undecorated wooden and metal toys are available from arts and crafts suppliers. Though often designed for decoupage, these can also be used with computer-printed output.

Decorating wood

The Paint It Wild™ Keepsake Chest (made by Balitono, Inc. and sold by Flax Art & Design) comes with a set of paints. But I decorated it by drawing colorful geometric designs in Illustrator, using a patterned fill to make the stripes. (To get the right sizes, I scanned the chest itself and imported the scan into Illustrator as a guide.) In order to leave plenty of space for the pretty wood grain to show, I arranged the designs to go around the small knobs on the drawers and also included clear star shapes. I printed the designs on a single sheet of Micro Format's Full Sheet Clear Photo Label paper, cut them out and applied them and was delighted to find that the lighter colors in the design also allowed some of the grain to show, making the labels look almost like inlaid or color-stained wood.

Letting white show through

Provo Craft makes white metal lunch boxes in several sizes, one of which is just right for storing postcards. I scanned it to use as a template in Photoshop and also scanned a sunset scene and sized it to fit. I boosted the saturation, added cyan to the image and applied Photoshop's Cutout filter to make the image look more like a silkscreen print. It's a style I saw used often on postcards from Switzerland (shown below the box). The type at the bottom of the photo image was white in Photoshop but when printed on Micro Format's self-adhesive Full Sheet Clear Photo Labels, the white areas of the type are transparent.

Using Lamination

Xyron, Inc. makes five lamination machines, three of which are four-in-one tools that can apply archival permanent adhesive, archival removable adhesive, protective lamination or magnet material. The Xyron 510 accommodates materials up to 5 inches wide and retails for about $100. (The Xyron 850 handles 8 1/2-inch widths and the Xyron 1200 handles widths up to 12 inches). All of the Xyron machines are hand-cranked, do not require heat, electricity or batteries and can be used to apply laminates, adhesive and magnets to any piece of paper, as well as to small thin objects such as dried flowers or leaves. The versatile Xyron system is used by crafters to create scrapbook pages, bookmarks, photo frames, refrigerator magnets and so on. Many of the projects in this book that were created by printing on special paper (see "Going Beyond Paper" on page 111) could also be made by printing on plain paper and then applying Xyron coatings.

Creating a weather-resistant banner

Out-of-town visitors sometimes have a hard time finding my driveway along our rural road. I thought of tying a wind sock to a tree, but realized that the Xyron 510 could help me create a custom-made driveway banner. Though the 510 handles items that are 5 inches wide or less, it can apply its coatings continuously for several feet, up to the length of the coating roll itself (which ranges from 5 feet for magnets to 18 feet for adhesives).

My multi-strip banner has an Asian theme. I started by cutting long strips from some scrap pieces of red and yellow paper. Then I chose black-and-white Japanese crest designs from *Oriental Designs: CD-ROM and Book* (Dover, 1999) and printed them on Micro Format's Super Color Designer Gold, a metallic inkjet paper. I re-sized them so they'd fit inside the 2-inch width of the paper strips. I also added red and yellow to the designs in Photoshop—using a scan of the two papers to match the color—and printed those. I cut out all the printed designs and glued them to the paper strips with a glue stick, also adding pieces of cut foil and origami paper. I carefully fed them two strips at a time through the Xyron 510, which was loaded with the two-sided lamination cartridge. I trimmed the strips so that some of the laminate overhangs the paper edges, punched holes in the tops of the strips, attached them to a stick with colored garden twine and hung the banner from a tree branch. The lamination provides protection from the damp Mendocino weather.

Gifts for Children

Paper has been used to make toys and games probably for as long as this versatile material has existed, creating a proliferation of board games, card games, paper dolls, coloring books, folded airplanes, hats, masks, puppets and jumping-jacks. Most of the toys in this chapter are made with ordinary paper, but some make use of new media for inkjet printers such as magnet sheets and jigsaw puzzle paper. The projects in this section require intermediate computer skills and are designed to be made by adults as gifts for children, or by children working with adult help.

Creating paper dolls

To make a paper doll, print a doll image on stiff, card-weight paper and cut it out with scissors. Dolls can also be printed on magnet sheets and used as refrigerator decorations or arranged on a baking sheet. There are several ways to create paper doll characters.

PHOTOS OF CHILDREN

Photograph a child wearing a bathing suit or underwear. Be sure to include the child's whole body in the photo and use

Scanning a real doll
To create a paper doll, I used one of my own childhood dolls, made in the 1950s. I took off her dress, placed her face down on my scanner, then edited the scan to remove some of her hair, trim her pantaloons and brighten her color.

Creating doll clothes
To make clothes for my doll, I started by scanning the fourteenth century Chief of the Parisian city militia from *Racinet's Full-Color Pictorial History of Western Costume* (Dover, 1987). In Photoshop I selected the Chief's helmet and enlarged it to fit my doll's head and also widened the Chief's outfit to fit her better. To add to my doll's wardrobe (opposite page), I also scanned the lacy Valentine dress in which the real doll was originally dressed. (I found it was better to scan the dress with the doll still inside it, to make it hold the right shape, and then selected and deleted the parts of the doll that were showing.) I also scanned my old Navaho doll, deleted her face and hands, and adapted her dress to fit my paper doll. This meant selecting and rotating the sleeves to fit my doll's arms.

a plain background if possible, so it's easier to silhouette the figure. (To remove the background see "Working with Selections" on page 36.)

CHILDREN'S DRAWINGS

Scan and print a child's drawing of a person.

REAL DOLLS

Scan a real doll, then clean up the scan and print. Small cloth, plastic, wooden or porcelain dolls can be placed face down on a scanner and scanned directly (see "Scanning Real Objects" on page 32). Larger dolls can be photographed with a digital camera or else conventional photo prints of them can be scanned.

HISTORICAL ART

Photos of historical dolls or figures in paintings can be scanned and used as paper dolls. Adults may enjoy creating contemporary clothing for Renaissance nudes.

Clothing for paper dolls

To create clothing to fit your doll, make your own drawings, or scan bits of fabric, or scan images from books of historical costume or try scanning actual doll clothes placed on your scanner. Take advantage of Photoshop's layers to position your scanned clothing over your doll figure and adjust its size and shape to fit. Add tabs to help your doll clothes stay on the doll and print them on lighter-weight paper.

Adding a child's face

To add my daughter Molly's face to the paper doll, I scanned one of her school photos, selected just her face and pasted it into a layer in Photoshop. I adjusted the color to match that of the doll, then carefully used the eraser tool with a feathered edge to remove the outside edges of the face so that it blended with that of the doll.

Mystery cards

Close-ups of familiar objects can be mysteriously hard to recognize. Take advantage of this to create two related card games: Mystery Lotto and Mystery Memory Game. Spend a day photographing interesting objects around your home. Using a digital camera will make the project easier. Get fairly close to each object, but include enough so it's easy to recognize. Take at least 24 pictures and make the images as large in size and resolution as possible. Use your image-editing program to crop each image to a square. Also select a much smaller square portion of each one and save this as a separate image. Now convert all the images, both the original photos and the close-ups, to the same size (for example, 3 inches square at 240 ppi). Now you're ready to create the games, using the guidelines below.

Creating memory cards

Print all 48 of your images (24 original photos and 24 close-ups) on card stock and cut them out. Now you have 24 pairs of images that are similar but not identical. Here are the rules: Spread all the cards face down across a table. Players take turns turning two cards over to see if they match. If the cards consist of a photo and its close-up, that's a match and the player can take those two cards out of play. If the cards don't match, they are turned face down again. As the game progresses, players must memorize the location of the cards so that they can turn over cards that match. The player with the most cards taken out of play wins.

Creating lotto game boards

Using your original photos, copy and paste them to create four different game boards with six images each. Print these on card stock. Then print all 24 of your close-up photos and cut them out to create cards. Now play a child's version of lotto. Shuffle the cards and let children take turns choosing cards and seeing if they can find a match on their game board. The fact that the images are not identical makes the game a little trickier and teaches children to look carefully at details.

Puzzles

New media for inkjet printers make it possible to create interesting puzzles.

JIGSAW PUZZLES

Compoz-A-Puzzle makes blank white jigsaw puzzles designed for decorating by hand with paint, pencil and so on. But now they also make Puzzle Clonzz inkjet printable puzzles that can be printed on any straight path printer. Micro Format makes iron-on transfer puzzles that come in greeting-card size with an envelope and also in a larger size. The card-size puzzle could be used as a party invitation.

MAGNET PUZZLES

Inkjet printable magnet sheets can be used to create magnetic puzzle pieces. In addition to the quilt squares shown here, magnet puzzles could be modeled on tangram shapes.

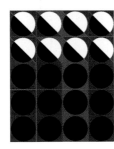

Making a jigsaw puzzle

To create the art for my puzzle, I scanned a piece of Central American mola embroidery. I wanted an image with lots of visual clues, but without a definite image. I printed the image on a Puzzle Clonzz inkjet printable puzzle from Compoz-a-Puzzle. The paper is pre-cut, but held together with small tabs until it's printed and punched apart. The paper is much thinner than a conventional puzzle and could easily be mailed in an envelope. To create a thicker jigsaw puzzle, try using an iron-on transfer puzzle from Micro Format, or use T-shirt transfer material to print an image onto one of Compoz-a-Puzzle's thicker blank puzzles.

Creating a magnetic quilt puzzle

Quilts are made up primarily of squares and diagonals combined in various patterns. I created a quilt-like puzzle by creating three sheets of quilt "pieces." To help organize the color scheme I used two pairs of complementary colors (double complements) plus black and white. I chose the colors from the 12-color wheel shown in "Working with Color" on page 54. After printing, I cut the squares out with scissors and arranged them on a magnet bulletin board. The brightly colored squares can make an interesting and ever-changing display in the kitchen, family room or office, as children and other passersby are inspired to rearrange them.

Custom board games

When we were kids, my brother and I played board games at home with each other and our friends and on holidays with our cousins and grandparents. I remember greatly enjoying the traditional games of checkers, Parcheesi, Chinese checkers, chess and the ever-popular, cut-throat American game of Monopoly.

HISTORICAL GAMES

But there are many more interesting board games—not easily available in stores—that have been played for thousands of years around the world. With a computer, scanner and printer, plus a book on historical games, you can create your own art for The Game of Goose, Snakes and Ladders, Alquerque, Go-Bang, Backgammon, and one of my favorites, Nine Men's Morris.

Using a photo background
Diagrams for Nine Men's Morris and sixteen other games are found in *Favorite Board Games You Can Make and Play* by Asterie Baker Provenzo and Eugene F. Provenzo, Jr. (Dover, 1981). The book explains how to make the games with paper, cardboard and craft tools, but the black-and-white diagrams can also be scanned and used as computer templates. I used Illustrator to make a simple version of the Nine Men's Morris board, then opened it in Photoshop and imported a digital photo as a background. A small game board can be made by gluing trimmed-letter-size prints onto poster board or foam core board.

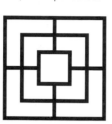

Decorating a game board
To create a more elaborate version of Nine Men's Morris, I used Illustrator to add solid color to my simple black-and-white diagram and to art of fruit and leaves imported from *1500 Decorative Ornaments: CD-ROM and Book* (Dover, 2000).

Creating a full-size game board
After creating my fruit and leaves board design in Illustrator, I opened the EPS in Photoshop at a size of 14 by 14 inches to match a store-bought game board. I copied the center square of the design and placed it in a separate document. Then I cropped the game board art down to one 7-inch by 7-inch corner section and printed four copies of it on glossy photo paper. I glued these onto a checkerboard that I bought at the drug store, leaving its red and black border still visible as a trim. Then I printed the center square and glued it down to cover the seams of the other paper. To play the game, I use the checkers that came with the board. This technique of printing in sections and gluing to a ready-made board can be used for any board game that uses a square format.

Creating a new chess board design is one of the easiest ways to learn to use a PostScript illustration program such as Illustrator, FreeHand or CorelDRAW. Tools for alignment help you to line up a row of squares, which can be filled with solid colors or with blended color gradients.

GAME INSTRUCTION BOOKLETS

Custom made game boards can be accompanied by a sheet of instructions for play, or even better, with a small pamphlet that explains the history of the game as well. For my Nine-Men's Morris game I created a cover with an illustration of children playing the game and inner pages printed on both sides with historical background and instructions. Pamphlets such as this could also be filled with instructions for various card games (such as pinochle) and given as a gift with a deck of cards. I made my game instruction pamphlet the same size as a standard large greeting card (5 by 7 inches) so it could be slipped into an A7 envelope.

Beyond black and red
It's easy to use a PostScript drawing program such as Adobe Illustrator to create chess and checkers boards with wild colors. For the design above I filled the background square with a linear gradient from green to purple, oriented on a diagonal. Then I used Illustrator's alignment tools to position 32 small squares in a grid of 8 rows and filled them as a group with a linear gradient from red to yellow. The color scheme is that of double complements— red and green plus yellow and purple. (See "Working with Color" on page 54 for information about color combinations.)

The design below uses radial gradients of yellow to green for the background and pink to yellow for the squares. But to give the design a kick I substituted black and white for the four squares at the center. Interesting chess board designs can function as graphic art pieces as well as game boards.

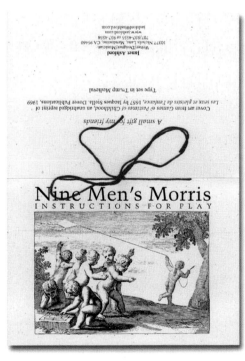

Making a game instruction booklet
I scanned an illustration of children playing Nine Men's Morris from *Games & Pastimes of Childhood*, a reprint of a 1657 French original (Dover, 1969) and used it for the cover of my game instruction booklet. The cover is printed on a single sheet of card stock, with the back cover text upside down so that it will be right side up when the sheet is folded in half. The inside sheet is printed on both sides and includes the rules for the game along with diagrams of the game board that I drew in Adobe Illustrator. I printed the booklet in black ink with my laser printer. After folding, it was sewn together with red embroidery thread using the 3-hole pamphlet stitch described on page 94.

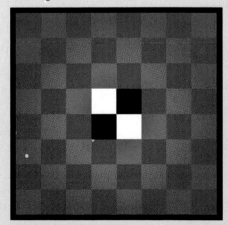

Making masks

Early human hunters wore masks during ceremonial dances to invoke the power of the animals they hunted. Remnants of this magic have come down to us in the decorative masks we wear for costume parties and Mardi Gras. Wearing a mask can free us to express emotions and actions that are forbidden and children especially enjoy the masquerade. The computer can be an aid in making masks of paper, or for making templates for masks of felt or other cloth. Look for sources of mask graphics in photographs of animals, in famous paintings or in books of monsters. You might like to add feathers, glitter or ribbons to your masks.

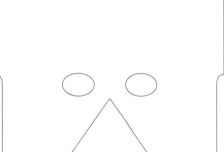

Victorian face masks

Look for heads of people or animals who are facing front, such as this cat and monkey from *500 Full-Color Decorative Illustrations: CD-ROM and Book* (Dover, 2000). I opened each one in Photoshop and placed it in a layer above my mask template. Then I increased the size and adjusted the proportions to make the animals fit. Because the monkey face was asymmetrical, I deleted the right half of it and copied and flipped the left half to make a mirror image. Likewise, because the cat's right whiskers droop, I deleted the right half of the cat's lower face and copied and flipped the left half to complete it. I then deleted the image inside the eye holes and selected and deleted the mouth, chin and neck of each face. Also, because I had to enlarge the small illustrations quite a lot, I applied the Median filter to smooth out the pixelation that had occurred with enlargement and also applied the Cutout filter to the monkey to simplify the color shapes. I printed the masks on card stock, punched holes in the sides and added string ties.

Creating a basic mask template

This basic template can be used as a guide for creating masks from any scanned source. First fold an 8 ½-inch by 11-inch piece of paper in half the short way and hold it to your face with the fold running up and down along your nose. Use a pen to mark the position of your eyes, the tops of your ears and the bridge of your nose. Use scissors to cut out an oval around each eye position, a slanted cut to leave room for your nose, and a slight indentation to create a projection above your ears (top, left). Scan the folded mask template and use it as a guide for drawing a neater version in Illustrator, FreeHand, or Photoshop (top, right). Then bring your finished template into Photoshop and copy and flip it along the horizontal axis to create a complete mask. This basic shape can now be filled with scanned artwork or photos to add color or images to your mask. For more mask shapes and ideas that can be adapted to computer work see *Paper Mask Making* by Michael Grater (Dover, 1984).

More Arts and Crafts Projects for Children

There are many delightful craft projects for children that can take advantage of photography, clip art, image-editing and the new media available for inkjet and laser printers (see "Going Beyond Paper" on page 111). Here are some of the many ideas I've had, but couldn't fit into this edition of *The Arts and Crafts Computer*. You can find more ideas in the craft books listed in the Resources section. Try some of these projects, using the techniques you've learned, and send photos of your finished work to me at the address listed at the back of this book. I'd love to see what you (both children and adults) are doing.

Cloth dolls

The same sources and techniques used for paper dolls (see pages 120–121) can be used to create graphics for cloth dolls and doll clothes. Either print directly on cloth or print on iron-on transfer paper and apply to cloth. Sew and fill with stuffing. (See "Working with Cloth" on pages 112–113.)

Spool dolls

Buy old wooden spools from a craft supplier, measure them and decorate them by printing clothes and faces on strips of sticker paper that you wrap around the spools. Glue buttons on top for hats.

Paper theater with actors

Create a folded stage from cardboard and decorate it with paint and computer-generated images. Create stand-up figures (such as the one on page 103) from clip art, family photos or old paintings, to serve as your actors.

Paper bag puppets

Use your computer to create faces, such as the ones for the masks on page 126. Glue or fasten them onto small brown paper bags.

Cootie-Catchers

This folded paper object is used as a fortune-telling device and most grade-school kids know how to make one. Find a template on the Internet and make your own custom Cootie-Catchers.

Paper wallets and purses

This is an old Japanese craft, used with heavyweight decorative papers. You can decorate wallets and purses with computer printed art or stickers.

Paper boxes and houses

Try photographing someone's head from four sides and the top, then print it on a paper box template (see page 128) to make a cube head. Try photographing your own house and making a folded paper version of it or scan children's drawings of houses and fold them to become three-dimensional. The box templates on page 128 can be used and adapted for these projects.

Origami

Traditional origami creatures and boxes can be folded from paper that's been decorated with the computer. Try unusual combinations, such as folding paper cranes from paper printed with landscapes or seascapes.

Lanterns and luminaria

Use your computer to scan or create a simple design, then print it and wrap the paper around a tin can which you've previously filled with water and frozen. Use the paper as a template for piercing holes in the can with a hammer and nail, making one hole every half inch or so along the lines of the design. Melt the ice and place a small candle inside the finished can.

Pinwheels

Print designs on both sides of a square. Cut in from each corner and fold four of the points into the center. Attach to a stick with a pin. You know how!

Paper airplanes

Scan the templates from a paper airplane book, then use your computer to add the decorations. Try unusual combinations, such as making paper airplanes from paper printed with photographs of the sky or trees.

Kites

Use your computer to create artwork for small decorative paper kites to hang indoors. For ideas and models, look for a book on oriental kite design.

Windsocks, flags and banners

Design a flag for your family, neighborhood or town. Print directly on cloth (see page 113) or use iron-on transfers to print onto plain cloth.

Optical toys and images

Use your computer to create images for traditional optical toys such as animation flip books, scrolling movies and zoetropes (moving picture toys).

Altered card decks

Scan the face cards from a traditional deck and substitute the faces of your friends and family for the kings, queens and jacks.

Face games

Print different eyes, noses and mouths on separate strips and assemble in funny combinations. Use clip art or family photos (see "Playing with the Past" on page 41) and include features from animals, monsters and angels.

Hats and crowns

Add computer-generated stickers or decals to folded paper hats, or fold small ones from computer-printed paper. Scan crowns from old paintings or clip art and print them on metallic paper. Decorate them with glitter and ribbons.

Magic wands

Create a fancy star, print two copies, glue them together over the end of a stick and add ribbon.

Fairy wings

Print decorative designs on metallic paper, cut into wing shapes and attach to a curved wire frame or print on transparency paper and attach to a fabric base that can be tied around the body.

A fairy wand and pinwheel in one!
This pinwheel wand was printed on card stock with a photo of flowers on one side and the same photo (altered with Photoshop's Glowing Edges filter) on the back. I added metallic edges with a gel pen from Flax Art & Design. Flax also supplied the Crazy Ribbon for the ties, which I combined with gift ribbon. The wheel is pinned to a twig with a small nail.

Creating Folded Boxes

Lovely, clever boxes can be folded from paper or card stock that's been printed with digital images. The only limitation is size: most boxes must be constructed from a letter-size or legal-size sheet. But box diagrams can often be divided into sections and the graphics printed onto more than one sheet and glued together to create larger boxes. Folded boxes can be used to enclose small presents (of jewelry, candy, money and so on). They can also be used as art objects in their own right. Boxes can be decorated with photos, scanned art work, clip art or scanned objects.

Boxes work best when folded from heavier weight, stiff paper. But in addition to card-weight paper, images for boxes can be printed on transparency film (for a see-through box), glossy photo paper and metallic paper. In addition, boxes can be cut and folded from decorative artist's paper and then decorated with stickers printed with digital images. There are many folded box forms available. A good selection of scannable templates is found in *Fantastic Folded Forms* (see Resources). In addition, Dover Publications and Hearst Books make decorated, punch out boxes which can be traced to create templates. Rubber Stampede makes kits of blank folded gift boxes. Pre-cut folded pyramid boxes are available from Nasco Arts & Crafts.

Using box templates

Below are templates for a four-petal box and a basic cube box, both of which can be printed on a single letter-size sheet of paper. The templates are printed here at 44 percent of actual size, so enlarge them to 227 percent to restore them to letter size. At full size the rectangle border of each one should be 8 $\frac{1}{2}$ inches by 11 inches. If you scan the templates into Photoshop, you can then add an image, such as a photo, in another layer and move it to fit the box outlines. It's also possible to autotrace scanned templates with Streamline and add color and designs in a PostScript illustration program such as Illustrator or FreeHand. The heavy outer line can be printed along with whatever images you include, to serve as a cutting guide. But be sure to select and delete the dashed folding lines before printing the images.

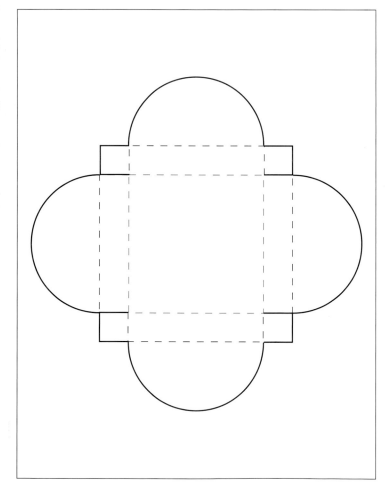

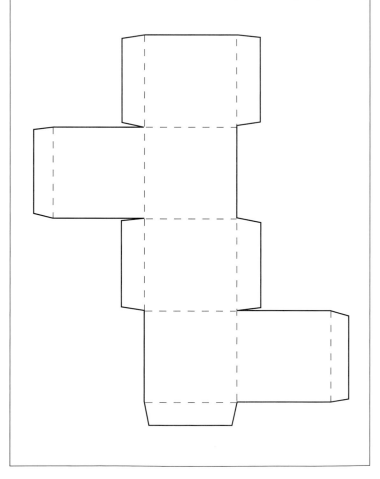

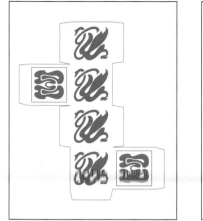   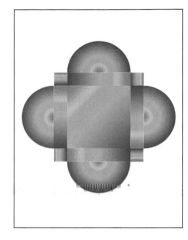

Printing and folding paper boxes

• To create a transparent box, I printed clip art on a piece of Ink Jet Transparency Film from RoyalBrites, using the cube box template on the opposite page. I glued it together with PVA glue, since this liquid glue dries clear when applied in thin coats.

• To create a slightly larger cube box, I enlarged the template and cut it into two parts, adding a flap to one of the sections. I placed a mandala design on each of the six faces and folded and glued the two pieces to create a box display for the art. (The mandala designs were created in Adobe Illustrator. See page 13 for more information.)

• Finally, I used Illustrator to fill the shapes of the four-petal box form with radial and linear gradients. I started with pastel shades of yellow, pink and blue. I then opened the Illustrator art in Photoshop and used the Hue/Saturation sliders to change the palette to hot pink, purple and turquoise, creating an instant box variation.

Using folded boxes

A transparent box (left) makes a nice container for a small gift wrapped in tissue paper. A four-petal box (front) also makes a nice gift package—one that can be used afterward as a decorative object.

A cube box printed on glossy photo paper (right) makes an interesting display object for family photos or art. (See page 131 for a cube box used as a Christmas tree ornament.)

Holidays Through the Year

Many of our familiar holidays occur at the same times of year as much older rituals having to do with nature and events of the agricultural calendar. Celebrating the seasons with special crafts and decorations can enhance our connection to natural cycles and is especially exciting for children. You might like to set aside a table top as a seasonal display area, on which to arrange leaves, flowers, fruits, candles and images of the season (some of which can be created using your computer). My favorite book for holiday ideas is one from England called *Festivals, Family and Food* by Diana Carey and Judy Large (Hawthorn Press, 1982). It includes this poem:

The Calendar

I knew when Spring was come
Not by the murmurous hum
Of bees in the willow-trees,
   Or frills
   Of daffodils,
Or the scent of the breeze;
But because there were whips and tops
By the jars of lollipops
In the two little village shops.

I knew when Summer breathed
Not by the flowers that wreathed
The sedge by the water's edge,
   Or gold
   Of the wold,
Or white and rose of the hedge;
But because, in a wooden box
In the window at Mrs. Mock's
there were white-winged shuttlecocks.

I knew when Autumn came
Not by the crimson flame
Of leaves that lapped the eaves
   Or mist
   In amethyst
And opal-tinted weaves;
But because there were alley-taws [marbles]
(Punctual as hips and haws)
On the counter at Mrs. Shaw's.

I knew when Winter swirled
Not by the whitened world
   Or silver skeins in the lanes,
   Or frost
That embossed
Its patterns on window-panes;
But because there were transfer-sheets
By the bottles of spice and sweets
In the shops in two little streets.
—Barbara Euphan Todd

Decorations for Celebrations

On these two pages I show only a few of the many arts and crafts possibilities for holidays and parties. Since our country is home to many religions and holiday traditions, I will leave it to you to consult the many fine books available on crafts and decorations for celebrations. But while looking for ideas, remember that your computer, scanner and printer can be put to good use with any projects that involve paper. Also take another look through this book to see which of the projects involving special media (such as transparencies, magnet sheets, iron-on transfers and so on) can be adapted to graphics for festivities.

Translucent shades

Cut paper designs are a traditional part of holiday and festival decorating all around the world. As Ernst Lehner says in *Alphabets and Ornaments*, "Since times of old, human beings were intrigued by an unbelievable bodily phenomenon around them, the shadow. Everywhere black shadows waxed and waned, painting grotesque shapes and figures on everything. No wonder that the creative mind … used light and shadow as an artistic and decorative medium." I found that cut paper designs can be adapted to computer use by being scanned and printed on translucent paper and curved into a tube to fit over a small tea light or candle. These small shades can be decorated with images to suit any occasion and used as glowing night time decorations for the table or a window sill.

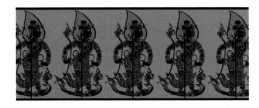

Using cut-paper designs

To create a decorative shade for a candle, I scanned a cut-paper Thai shadow puppet design from *Alphabets and Ornaments* by Ernst Lehner (Dover, 1952), which also includes beautiful cut-paper examples from Japan, China, India, Java, Turkey, Egypt, Russia, Holland, Italy, Vienna, Switzerland and Germany.

I flipped the puppet across the horizontal axis to make a mirror image, because it would be printed on back lit film, which is viewed from the opposite side. Then I copied and repeated it to fill a 10-inch width and added black borders to the top and bottom of the 4-inch high strip. I added color to the white spaces in the design and printed the art on Canon's Back Print Film, a mylar film with a translucent white printing surface, designed for rear illumination. Remember that photographs and other images that are not symmetrical should be flipped to a mirror image so they can be viewed from the glossy non-printed side of the film.

Christmas tree ornaments

Though my spiritual life has evolved away from Christianity over the years, I was raised in that tradition and the Christmas holiday is still for me a time of richness and beauty. My collection of Christmas decorations has become a treasure trove of memories, as every December I see again the many special ornaments given to me by my friends and my mother (who always bought ornaments for me on her travels) as well as the ones made by my children at school, the ones I made myself and the tatted snowflakes bought at church bazaars. I hope that you have in your life a religious or spiritual faith that gives you peace, beautiful and inspiring images, a connection with the past and a sense of home.

Computer Crafts for Celebrations

Your computer, scanner and color printer can be tools for making many good-looking gifts and decorations for holidays and parties. Many of the traditional crafts featured in craft books and magazines can be adapted for use with computer printed images. Here are some examples:

- stickers for Easter eggs
- place cards for Thanksgiving dinner
- folded paper May baskets
- centerpieces for holiday meals
- party invitations
- decorative place mats
- party bags
- Valentines
- Christmas tree ornaments
- Small decorative dioramas with stand-up figures (such as a Christmas manger scene, a Thanksgiving pilgrim scene, and so on)

Creating a box ornament

The cube box template shown on page 128 can be used to create a folded box ornament. I decorated mine (and the other ornaments on this page) with Victorian images from *Full-Color Decorative Christmas Illustrations: CD-ROM and Book* (Dover, 1999). You could also use snowflake designs or scans of cut paper designs. I added a gold square behind each image and a solid red background, to provide a frame that ties all the illustrations together. I printed my ornament on glossy photo paper, which is stiff enough to make a sturdy box. You could also experiment with printing on metallic papers, or you could fold your box from handmade, decorative paper and then apply the images as stickers.

Creating a flat paper ornament

To create a flat paper cutout ornament, print two copies of any Christmas image, but make sure one of them is flipped to be a mirror image of the other. After printing, carefully cut around them, making sure the edges match and then glue them together back to back with a piece of ribbon or yarn glued into the top as a hanger. I printed my angel on slightly metallic Super Color Pearl Essence paper from Micro Format and my Santa on photo glossy paper from Epson. I cut the Santa close to the edges of the image, but left a wide border of pearly paper around the figure of the angel.

Gift Certificates

Small gift-wrapped boxes and decorated bags are perfect for enclosing gift certificates, making a sometimes last-minute idea seem special. You can enclose money or a gift certificate to a local book or music store or make your own gift certificates for services you provide. Such personal presents are especially appreciated by busy working parents and elderly people. Ideas include:

- a massage
- a pedicure
- a session at the sauna
- a horoscope or tarot reading
- an evening of baby-sitting
- help with walking the dog
- watering and weeding the garden
- taking out the trash
- washing the dishes
- house-sitting
- splitting and stacking firewood
- dinner out and a movie
- afternoon tea for two
- a chess game at the coffeehouse

Gift Wrapping

Making wrapping paper

As long as you have a scanner and a color printer you'll never be at a loss for wrapping paper, at least for small gifts. Any sort of colorful objects, papers or photos can be scanned and printed on a single sheet of letter-size paper and used to wrap items the size of a music CD or a small box (see "Images from Everywhere" on page 133 for ideas). For larger gifts, try printing on legal size paper or continuous feed banner paper or print several sheets and tape or glue them together.

Creating wrapping paper

The Mexican Loteria game includes charming and colorful images that can be scanned to make wrapping paper, gift bags, stickers and gift cards. I scanned El Pescado, enlarged it to fill an entire letter-size sheet and wrapped a small box. I also scanned several Loteria game boards to create a sheet covered with a smaller pattern. I used it to wrap a music CD and tied the package with metallic red and gold Crazy Ribbon from Flax Art & Design.

Creating a gift bag

A single letter-size sheet can be folded to make a small gift bag. Simply fold it around an empty box (such as the kind that bank checks come in) and seal one end, leaving the other end open. Then remove the box and add tissue paper and your present. I used a hole punch to make holes in the top edges and added yarn handles to my bag. Placing a piece of cardboard in the bottom of the paper bag will make it stronger.

Stickers on bags
I scanned three Lotería cards at three different enlargements to match the sizes of a handmade gift tag and two plain colored gift bags purchased at a craft store. I printed the card images on sticker paper, trimmed them with scissors, applied them to the bags and card and *voilá*. I could also have printed them on plain paper and applied adhesive using a Xyron laminating machine.

Images from Everywhere

The thrift store, used book store and your own home, office, junk drawer, street and backyard can be rich sources for decorative images to print and apply to gift wrapping as well as to recycled items such as the cans and bottles shown on pages 116–117. Try scanning or photographing some of the everyday objects and artifacts around you, using both long shots and extreme close-ups. Develop an eye for color and pattern. A Persian style carpet or a summer rose (below) can be printed and used as wrapping paper or incorporated into any of the other projects in this chapter.

- almost anything from a store in a Chinese, Japanese, East Indian or Mexican neighborhood
- ethnic cloth and embroideries
- feathers
- flowers
- lace
- leaves
- maps
- pages from old books
- painted dishes
- playing cards
- postage stamps
- small toys
- tickets

Decorating gift bags

Ready-made plain gift bags with handles are available in solid colors in stationery and craft stores. They can be decorated by applying stickers and attaching gift tags and ribbons. Colorful tissue paper completes the festive look. Stickers printed with digital images can also be used to create matching "party bags" for holding small presents and treats for guests at a children's party. You can use the small colored party bags sold in stationery stores or simple brown paper lunch bags.

Creating gift tags

Small gift tags can be made by printing directly on card-weight paper or by printing on sticker paper and then attaching the stickers to folded blank cards. It's nice to create gift tags with images that match the graphics on your wrapping paper or bag, but are slightly different. Also, if you're wrapping a gift that you made using one of the techniques in this book, you might want to create wrapping paper and tags that match or complement the graphics on the gift.

Resources

Books on Traditional Arts and Crafts

Art safety
Health Hazards Manual for Artists
Michael McCann, Ph.D., CIH
Lyons and Burford, 1994

Making Art Safely
Merle Spandorfer, Deborah Curtiss, and Jack Snyder, MD
Van Nostrand Reinhold, 1993

Book arts
Bookworks: Making Books by Hand
Gwenyth Swain with the Minnesota Center for the Book Arts
Carolrhoda Books, 1997

Books Don't Have to be Flat
Kathy Pike and Jean Mumper
Scholastic Professional Books, 1998

Cover to Cover: Creative Techniques for Making Beautiful Books, Journals & Albums
Shereen LaPlantz
Lark Books, 1995
Clear diagrams and instructions plus beautiful color photos of finished projects, from a well-known American book artist.

Creative Bookbinding
Pauline Johnson
Dover Publications, 1963
Excellent basic techniques for bookbinding, book repair and paper decorating. Many book structures, examples and creative ideas.

Easy-to-Make Decorative Boxes and Desk Accessories
Annette Hollander
Dover Publications, 1986
Basic bookbinding techniques for making paper hinges, boxes, albums, portfolios, slip cases and so on.

Making Books by Hand
Mary McCarthy and Philip Manna
Quarry Books, North Light Books, 1997
Clear instructions, color photos of each step, plus beautiful color photos of finished books by well-known book artists.

Making Books That Fly, Fold, Wrap, Hide, Pop Up, Twist and Turn (Books for Kids to Make)
Gwen Deihn
Lark Books, 1998

Making Journals by Hand: 20 Creative Projects for Keeping Your Thoughts
Jason Thompson
Rockport Publishers, 2000

Non-Adhesive Binding: Books without Paste or Glue
Keith A. Smith
Published by Keith A. Smith
22 Cayuga Street
Rochester, NY 14620-2153
716/473-6776
The definitive source, from a master bookbinder, on binding books with only folding and stitching, including many Japanese methods.

Color palettes and color theory
Color Harmony Series
Rockport Publishers
A recent series of seven color harmony books that include color wheels and samples, photos, color swatch combinations and CMYK components.

The Designer's Guide to Color Combinations: 500+ Historic and Modern Color Formulas in CMYK
Leslie Cabarga
North Light, 1999

Paper and paper crafts
The Art of Money: The History and Design of Paper Currency from Around the World
David Standish
Chronicle Books, 2000
Full-color examples of beautiful paper currency.

The Complete Origami Course
Paul Jackson
Gallery Books
W. H. Smith Publisher Inc., 1989
From England, clear instructions for animals, toys, boxes and so on.

The Crafter's Project Book: 80+ Projects to Make and Decorate
Mary Ann Hall and Sandra Salamony
Quarry, Rockport Publishers, 2000

Crafting with Handmade Paper: Great Projects to Make with Beautiful Papers
Gail Hercher
Quarry, Rockport Publishers, 2000
Beautiful projects including invitations, journals and envelopes.

Creating with Paper: Basic Forms and Variations
Pauline Johnson
Dover Publications, 1991
Reprint of a charming 1958 original on creating art forms with solid colored paper.

Creative Paper Art: Techniques for Transforming the Surface
Nancy Welch
Sterling Publishing Co., 1999
Luscious photos and clear instructions for decorating paper using marbling, splattering, sponging, folding, rubbing, paste paper, dyeing, gilding, embossing, sewing, weaving, plus instruction for boxes, bags, and an accordion-fold book.

Decoupage: Original Ideas for More Than 50 Quick and Easy Designs to Make in a Weekend
Juliet Bawden
Lark Books, 1996
From England, a variety of decoupage projects for the home, all of which could be made with computer generated patterns and papers.

Fantastic Folded Forms: Patterns for Boxes, Envelopes and Unusual Forms
Bets Cole
Letterlines
89477 Sheffler Road
Elmira, OR 97437
541/935-3505
Clear, easy-to-scan patterns for over 25 different box shapes and 3 envelopes.

Greeting Card Magic with Rubber Stamps
MaryJo McGraw
North Light Books, 2000

Kirigami: Fun with Paper Folding and Cutting
Heian International
Torrance, CA 90501
A series of 8 small books, each with kirigami paper included.

Make Your Own Decorative Boxes with Easy-To-Use Patterns
Karen Kjaeldgard-Larsen
Dover Publications, 1995
Instructions and templates for making boxes of cardboard, pasteboard and heavy paper, covered with decorative papers.

Making Memory Boxes: Box Projects to Make, Give, and Keep
Barbara Mauriello
Rockport Publishers, 2000
Beautiful ideas for handmade boxes and book forms.

Origami: From Angelfish to Zen
Peter Engel
Dover Publications, 1989
A fascinating, illustrated 75-page introduction and history of the art and symbolism of Origami, followed by clear instructions for many forms.

Paper Perfect: 25 Bright Ideas for Paper
Labena Ishaque
Lark Books, 1998

Papermaking: The History and Technique of an Ancient Craft
Dard Hunter
Dover Publications, 1978
(reprint of 1947 original)

Simply Super Paper: Over 50 Projects to Cut, Curl, Twist, and Tease from Paper
Sandra Lounsbury Foose
Contemporary Books, 2000

Books on Digital Arts

Computer graphics techniques

Adobe Press Classroom in a Book series
This series of textbook-style books with CD-ROM provides step-by-step tutorials that lead you through the tools and functions of Adobe software including Illustrator and Photoshop. Distributed by Peachpit Press.

Bert Monroy: Photorealistic Techniques with Photoshop and Illustrator
Bert Monroy
New Riders Publishing, 2000
A veteran computer illustrator reveals his techniques for creating striking, almost photographic still life and street scenes.

Creative Digital Printmaking: A Photographer's Guide to Professional Desktop Printing
Theresa Airey
Watson-Guptill, 2001

Design Essentials
Luanne Seymour Cohen
Adobe Press, 1999

Photoshop 6 Down and Dirty Tricks
Scott Kelby
NAPP Publishing, 2000
www.downanddirtytricks.com
www.scottkelby.com
From the founder of the National Association of Photoshop Professionals, this well-designed and illustrated book offers easy-to-follow, step-by-step tutorials.

Real World Scanning and Half-tones
David Blatner, Steve Roth, Glenn Fleishman
Peachpit Press, 1998

Start with a Digital Camera: A Guide to Using Digital Cameras to Create High-Quality Graphics
John Odam
Peachpit Press, 1999

Start with a Scan: A Guide to Transforming Scanned Photos and Objects into High-Quality Art, 2nd edition
Janet Ashford and John Odam
Peachpit Press, 2000
This book works very well as a supplement to *The Arts and Crafts Computer*, providing many examples of how to transform scanned photos, objects and art into images that can be printed and used in crafts projects.

Visual QuickStart Guide series
from Peachpit Press
Includes excellent, easy to follow guides to all the most popular graphics software including Photoshop, Illustrator, FreeHand, PageMaker and QuarkXPress.

Wow! Book series
A very good, award-winning series from Peachpit Press on the bestselling graphics software.
• **The Illustrator 9 Wow! Book**
Sharon Steuer, Steven H. Gordon and Sandra Alves
Peachpit Press, 2001
• **The Painter 6 Wow! Book**
Cher Threinen-Pendarvis
Peachpit Press, 2000
• **The Photoshop 6 Wow! Book**
Linnea Davis and Jack Davis
Peachpit Press, 2002

Computer graphics publishers

Peachpit Press
1249 Eighth Street
Berkeley, CA 94710
800/283-9444
www.peachpit.com
Request a catalog of Peachpit's excellent list of computer related books. Peachpit also distributes the Adobe Press books.

Graphic design

Design Writing Research: Writing on Graphic Design
Ellen Lupton and J. Abbott Miller
Princeton Architectural Press, 1996
Beautifully designed and illustrated, with intellectual, esoteric and stimulating essays on the history and future of type and design.

A History of Graphic Design
Philip B. Meggs
Van Nostrand Reinhold, 1983
This excellent illustrated 500+ page volume covers the invention of writing, medieval manuscript, origins of printing, graphic design, photography in design, Art Nouveau and Modernism.

Clip Art Crazy
Chuck Green
Peachpit Press, 1996
Clip art projects, a directory of companies and a CD-ROM with 500 images.

Design Through Discovery: An Introduction to Art and Design, 6th ed.
Marjorie Elliott Bevlin
Harcourt, Brace, 1994
Used as a college design textbook since 1963, this book includes a thorough overview of design principles and provides applications to all the arts and crafts.

The Desktop Publisher's Idea Book: One-of-a-kind Projects, Expert Tips, and Hard-to-find Sources
Chuck Green
Random House, 1998

Get Noticed: Self-Promotion for Creative Professionals
Sherre L. Clark and Kristen Lennert
North Light, 2000

Looking Good in Print: A Guide to Basic Design for Desktop Publishing
Roger C. Parker
Ventana Press, 1996
www.rcparker.com

The Non-Designer's Design Book: Design and Typographic Principles for the Visual Novice
Robin Williams
Peachpit Press, 1994

Seasonal Promotions
Poppy Evans
North Light, 1997
150 graphic design projects geared towards holidays

Visual Thinking: Methods for Making Images Memorable
Henry Wolf
American Showcase, 1988
Lavish color book of design ideas from a well-known New York photographer and art director for magazines and ad campaigns.

Type and typography

Adobe Type Library Reference Book
Adobe Systems Inc.
www.adobe.com
Written in English, French and German, this useful book includes background on the different classes of type and samples of all the PostScript type sold by Adobe—over 400 typeface families.

The Chicago Manual of Style
The University of Chicago Press
Since 1906 this has been a standard reference on language usage in publishing for writers, editors, typographers, printers and proofreaders. This is the book to consult when you're wondering whether to use a colon or a semicolon.

The Elements of Typographic Style
Robert Bringhurst
Hartley & Marks, 1992
A well-designed and beautifully written book from a man who is a poet and a typographer.

How to Boss Your Fonts Around
Robin Williams
Peachpit Press, 1998
Everything you need to know about font technology and font management on the Mac.

The Non-Designer's Type Book
Robin Williams
Peachpit Press, 1998

Printing and graphic production

Getting It Printed: How to Work With Printers and Graphic Imaging Services to Assure Quality, Stay on Schedule and Control Costs
Mark Beach and Eric Kenly
North Light Books, 1999

Great Production by Design: The Technical Know-How You Need to Let Your Design Imagination Soar
Constance J. Sidles
North Light Books, 1998

The Non-Designer's Scan and Print Book: All You Need to Know About Production and Prepress to Get Great-looking Pages
Sandee Cohen and Robin Williams
Peachpit Press, 1999

Pocket Pal: A Graphic Arts Production Handbook
Michael H. Bruno
GATF Press, 2000
Order from
GATF/PIA Publications
P.O. Box 1020
Sewickly, PA 15143-1020
800/662-3916
or
International Paper Print Resources Group
P.O. Box 770067
Memphis, TN 38177
800/854-3212

Computer Hardware and Software

Magazines

Book arts

The Book Arts Classified
Page Two, Inc.
Box 77167
Washington, DC 20013
800/821-6604
$16 per year
A newsletter for the book arts community, listing conferences, classes, and so on.

Graphic design

Before & After: How to Design Cool Stuff
2007 Opportunity Drive, Suite 10
Roseville, CA 95678-3005
916/784-3880
www.pagelab.com
No longer published, but 30 back issues are available for $12 each or $149 for all. Excellent how-to articles on computer graphics, illustration and design.

Communication Arts
410 Sherman Avenue
Palo Alto, CA 94306
800/258-9111
www.commarts.com
Showcase for the best work being done by top art directors, designers, illustrators and photographers.

Dynamic Graphics Magazine
Bimonthly
600 N. Forest Park Drive
Peoria, IL 61614
800/255-8800
www.dgusa.com
Great computer how-to magazine for "non-designers" with tips and projects for good type and design plus many craft ideas.

Computers

Apple Corporation
1 Infinite Loop
Cupertino, CA 95014
408/996-1010
800/538-9696, referral center
www.apple.com

Compaq Computer Corporation
20555 SH 249
Houston, TX 77070-2698
800/ATCOMPAQ
www.compaq.com

Dell Computer Corporation
One Dell Way
Round Rock, TX 78682
800/WWW-DELL
www.dell.com

Gateway
P.O. Box 2000
610 Gateway Drive
North Sioux City, SD 57049
800/846-2000
www.gateway.com

IBM (International Business Machines)
New Orchard Road
Armonk, NY 10504.
914/499-1900
www.ibm.com

Digitizing tablets

Wacom Technology Corporation
1311 SE Cardinal Court
Vancouver, WA 98683
800/922-9348
www.wacom.com

Scanners

Epson
3840 Kilroy Airport Way
Long Beach, CA 90806
800/873-7766
www.epson.com

Hewlett Packard
3000 Hanover Street
Palo Alto, CA 94304
650/857-5518
www.hewlettpackard.com

Microtek Lab Inc.
3715 Doolittle Drive
Redondo Beach, CA 90278
800/654-4160
www.microtekusa.com

UMAX Technologies
3561 Gateway Blvd.
Freemont, CA 94538
510/651-4000
www.umax.com

Digital cameras

Canon USA
1 Canon Plaza
Lake Success, NY 11042
516/328-5960
www.usa.canon.com

Eastman Kodak Company
343 State St.
Rochester, NY 14650
800/235-6325
www.kodak.com

Nikon
1300 Walt Whitman Road
Melville, NY 11747
800/645-6689
www.nikonusa.com

Olympus America Inc.
Two Corporate Center Drive
Melville, NY 11747-3157
631/844-5000
www.olympusamerica.com

Sony
550 Madison Avenue, 33rd floor
New York, New York 10022-3211
800/571-7669
www.sonystyle.com

Printers

Epson
3840 Kilroy Airport Way
Long Beach, CA 90806
800/873-7766
www.epson.com

Hewlett Packard
3000 Hanover Street
Palo Alto, CA 94304
650/857-5518
www.hewlettpackard.com

Computer software

Adobe Systems, Inc.
345 Park Avenue
San Jose, CA 95110
408/536-6000
www.adobe.com
Makers of Photoshop, Illustrator, PageMaker, InDesign, Streamline and PostScript fonts.

Corel Corporation
1600 Carling Avenue
Ottawa, Ontario K1Z 8R7, Canada
613/728-8200
www.corel.com
Makers of Painter, CorelDRAW, CorelPHOTO-PAINT, WordPerfect, KPT (Photoshop Plug-in effects), Bryce.

Macromedia
600 Townsend Street
San Francisco, CA 94103
415/252-2000
www.macromedia.com
Makers of FreeHand

Quark, Inc.
1800 Grant Street
Denver, CO 80203
307/772-7100
www.quark.com
Makers of QuarkXPress

Plug-In filters for Photoshop

Andromeda Software
699 Hampshire Road, Suite 109
Thousand Oaks, CA 91361
805/379-4109
www.andromeda.com
Filters for photography, 3D, mezzotints and textures.

Auto F/X
31 Inverness Center Parkway, Suite 270
Birmingham, AL 35242
888/828-8639
www.autofx.com
Plug-in filters that apply edge treatments to images and type.

KPT filters
Corel
1600 Carling Avenue
Ottawa, Ontario K1Z 8K7
Canada
www.corel.com
Kai's Power Tools plug-ins for Photoshop.

Digital type

Adobe Systems Inc.
345 Park Avenue
San Jose, CA 95110-2704
408/536-6000
www.adobe.com

Bitstream, Inc.
215 First Street
Cambridge, MA 02142
617/497-6222
www.bitstream.com

Emigre
4475 D Street
Sacramento, CA 95819
800/944-9021
www.emigre.com
New wave fonts plus a magazine, T-shirts and music.

Font Bureau
326 A Street, Suite 6C
Boston, MA 02210
617/423-8770
www.fontbureau.com

Hoefler Type Foundry
600 Broadway, Room 729
New York, NY 10012-2608
212/777-6640
www.typography.com
A fine collection of PostScript and TrueType fonts in Old and Modern styles.

House Industries
1145 Yorklyn Road
Yorklyn, DE 19736-0166
302/234-2356
www.houseindustries.com
Clever and well-designed retro and new wave fonts, provided in themed sets with matching special packaging and T-shirts; also music.

ITC (International Typeface Corporation)
200 Ballardvale Street
Wilmington, MA 01887-1069
866/823-5828
www.itcfonts.com
Over 1,000 classic and modern typefaces; publishes U&lc (Upper and Lower Case) magazine on-line.

Phil's Fonts
14605 Sturtevant Road
Silver Spring, MD 20905
301/879-6955
www.philsfonts.com
www.garagefonts.com
Traditional, geometric, amorphous, ironic, historic, handwritten and "destructive" typefaces; dealer for GarageFonts.

Reviews of computers, software and peripherals

Computing Review
www.computingreview.com
Product reviews plus message boards and a marketplace for used equipment.

Consumer Reports On-Line
www.consumerreports.com
This subscription service provides on-line access to all the product reviews done by Consumer's Union. Costs about $25 per year.

ZDNet
www.zdnet.com
Source for product reviews and links to Macworld and PCWorld magazines.

On-line ordering

Deal Time
www.dealtime.com
For any given computer product, Deal Time provides a list with links to on-line stores that sell it and their prices.

MacZone and PCZone
www.zones.com
These stores also provide printed color catalogs by mail.

Outpost
www.outpost.com
Sellers of computer and electronics equipment.

Digital stock photos and images

Artbeats Software, Inc.
P.O. Box 709
Myrtle Creek, OR 97457
800/444-9392
www.artbeats.com

Classic PIO Partners
87 East Green Street, Suite 309
Pasadena, CA 91105
800/370-2746
626/564-8106 in California
www.classicpartners.com

Comstock Images
244 Sheffield Street
Mountainside, NJ 07092
800/225-2722
www.comstock.com

Dynamic Graphics
6000 N. Forest Park Drive
Peoria, IL 61614
800/255-8800
www.dgusa.com

EyeWire
8 South Idaho Street
Seattle, WA 98134
800/661-9410
www.eyewire.com

PhotoDisc
701 North 34th Street, Suite 400
Seattle, WA 98103
800/528-3472
www.photodisc.com

RubberBall Productions
102 South Mountain Way Drive
Orem, UT 84058
888/224-3472
www.rubberball.com

Clip Art and Royalty Free Images

Printed clip art

Art Direction Book Company
456 Glenbrook Road
Stamford, CT 06906
203/353-1441

Dover Publications
31 East 2nd Street
Mineola, NY 11501
store.doverpublications.com
Dover publishes hundreds of books of clip art in both black-and-white and color, and also a number of collections on CD-ROM, providing thousands of images overall. Write for a catalog of Dover's Pictorial Archives Series.

Stemmer House Publishers
2627 Caves Road
Owings Mills, MD 21117-2998
410/363-3690
www.stemmer.com
Black-and-white clip art from around the world, with an emphasis on hand drawings based on folk art and designs taken from textiles and pottery. Includes some ethnic areas not covered by Dover, including Armenia and the Near East, Persia, the South Pacific, ancient Scandinavia, Poland and the Hmong people.

Clip art on CD-ROM

Direct Imagination
P.O. Box 93018
Pasadena, CA 91109-3018
888/793-8387
www.dimagin.com
Direct Imagination publishes the complete, full-color 1856 edition of the *Grammar of Ornament* by Owen Jones, with over 2,300 classic copyright-free designs; also *Art Nouveau Flowers and Plants*, *Costumes of China and Japan* (from Racinet's *Le Costume Historique*), and *Father of Industrial Design* featuring the work of Christopher Dresser. Most images are scans in TIFF format, but many have also been redrawn in EPS format and can be edited in Illustrator or FreeHand.

Dover Electronic Clip Art
See listing under "Printed Clip Art"
Dover's CD-ROM clip-art collections include scanned color art in TIFF format as well as black-and-white clip art with each piece provided in TIFF, EPS, GIF, JPEG and BMP formats.

Traditional Art Supplies and Papers

Many of the suppliers listed here also maintain Web sites that include craft ideas and projects.

Art supplies

Aiko's Art Materials Import
3347 North Clark Street
Chicago, IL 60657
773/404-5600
Japanese art materials including brushes, watercolors, Sumi inks, cutting tools, books, bookbinding supplies and papers.

Amsterdam Art
1013 University Avenue
Berkeley, CA 94710
510/549-4800
www.amsterdamart.com
Fine art and graphics supplies, discount prices, art classes, yearly trade show.

Collage
240 Valley Drive
Brisbane, CA 94005-1206
800/926-5524
www.collagecatalog.com
A specialized division of Flax Art and Design featuring blank books, artist papers, inks and pens, books, ribbon and cord, nesting boxes, stickers, seals, vellum envelopes and sheets.

Daniel Smith
4150 First Avenue South
Seattle, WA 98124-5568
800/426-6740
www.danielsmith.com
Fine quality art supplies and papers, including sample packs and fine arts digital papers. $5 for reference catalog or call to request a free sale catalog. Check Web site for technical information on artist materials.

Dick Blick Art Material
P.O. Box 1267
Galesburg, IL 61402-1267
800/828-4548
www.dickblick.com
Fine arts supplies and papers. Call 800/447-8192 for a free, 480-page catalog.

Flax Art & Design
240 Valley Drive
Brisbane, CA 94005-1206
888/352-9278
www.flaxart.com
Arts-related gifts, art supplies and craft kits.

NASCO Arts and Crafts
901 Janesville Avenue
Fort Atkinson, WI 53538-0901
and
4825 Stoddard Road
Modesto, CA 95356-9318
800/558-9595
www.nascofa.com
Extensive selection of supplies with special products for art teachers.

Sinopia
3385 22nd Street
San Francisco, CA 94110
415/824-3180
www.sinopia.com
Pigments and materials for fine arts.

Specialty papers

Encore Exotica
Apple Tree Lane
801 La Honda Road
Woodside, CA 94062
Charming packet of decorative old papers, images and scrap for collage. $12 postpaid from Apple Tree Lane.

Fascinating Folds
P.O. Box 10070
Glendale, AZ 85318
800/968-2418
www.fascinating-folds.com
Origami paper, books and supplies plus artisan papers and supplies for book binding, card-making, collage, decoupage, marbling, paper sculpture, pop-up and quilling.

Maziarczyk Paperworks
882 Stark Avenue
Niskayuna, NY 12309
518/374-5325
104 light-fast paste paper designs on acid-free paper.

New York Central
62 Third Avenue
New York, NY 10003
800/950-6111
www.nycentralart.com
Fine art, decorative and handmade papers from around the world plus tools, book-binding supplies, adhesives and archival products.

The Paper Catalog
240 Valley Drive
Brisbane, CA 94005-1206
888/727-3763
www.flaxart.com
Natural fiber, textured and marbled paper, tissue, decorative printed paper, lace, vellum, Japanese papers, gift wrap, stationery and envelopes.

Tibetan Collection from dZi
5778 2nd Street, NE
Washington, DC 20011
800/318-5857
www.dzi.com
Handmade papers from Tibet, in sheets, stationery packs, lanterns and so on. Products are fair traded from Tibetan refugee artisans and proceeds benefit the Tibetan Government in exile.

Recycled and tree-free papers

Green Earth Office Supply
P.O. Box 719
Redwood Estates, CA 95044
800/327-8449
www.greenearthofficesupply.com
Provides environmentally-friendly office supplies and papers, including a Treefree Sampler Pack

Green Field Paper Company
1330 G Street
San Diego, CA 92101
619/338-9432
www.greenfieldpaper.com
Makers of beautiful plain and decorative papers from hemp, coffee, garlic, junk mail, flower seeds, organic cotton and recycled post-consumer waste. Order a Deluxe Paper Sample Kit.

Green Mountain Desktop Supply
P.O. Box 1025
Alton, IL 62002
618-466-6311
www.greenmt.com
Provides hemp in letter-size reams, sketchpads, and various artist papers. Sample packs are available.

ReThink Paper
c/o Earth Island Institute
300 Broadway, Suite 28
San Francisco, CA 94133-3312
415/788-3666 Ex. 232
www.rethinkpaper.org
Resources on how paper can be made without cutting too many trees.

Treecycle Recycled Paper
P.O. Box 5086
Bozeman, MT 59717
406/586-5287
www.treecycle.com
Recycled paper plus links and environmental news and action alerts.

Craft and bookbinding tools

Bookmakers
6001 66th Avenue, Suite 101
Riverdale, MD 20737
301/459-3384
Sellers of the Kutrimmer Ideal Cutter, an excellent German paper cutter, as well as other tools for book binding.

C-Thru Ruler
www.cthruruler.com
Makers of rulers of all kinds, drafting tools, stencils, plastic templates for making folded paper boxes, bags and envelopes, scrapbooking tools and supplies.

Design a Card
P.O. Box 5314
Englewood, FL 34224
941/475-1121
www.artdeckle.com
Art Deckle metal ruler, embossing stylus, corner design templates for decorative paper corners.

Fascinating Folds
P.O. Box 10070
Glendale, AZ 85318
800/968-2418
www.fascinating-folds.com
Origami paper, books and supplies, artisan papers, supplies for bookbinding, card making, collage, decoupage, marbling, paper sculpture, pop-up, quilling.

Light Impressions
P.O. Box 22708
Rochester, NY 14692-2708
800/828-6216
www.lightimpressionsdirect.com
Archival albums, mats and frames, storage and presentation tools.

Rubber stamps

Retro Rubber Stamps
2960 Butte Street
Hayward, CA 94541
www.retro.to
Rubber stamps and accessories from Chris Rolik, a fine arts restorer and book artist.

Stamp Affair
500 Park Avenue, Suite 207
Lake Villa, IL 60046
847/265-3330
www.stampaffair.com
Rubber stamp catalog includes many craft techniques.

Supplies for Computer Printing

Avery Dennison Corp.
50 Pointe Drive
Brea, CA 92821
800/462-8379
www.avery.com
Cards, labels, static cling window material, clear adhesive sheets, magnet sheets, T-shirt transfers, banner paper, shrink sheets, canvas.

C-Thru Ruler —

Canon USA
1 Canon Plaza
Lake Success, NY 11042
516/328-5960
consumer.usa.canon.com
Artist canvas, Back Print Film, banner paper, magnet sheets, T-shirt transfer and fabric sheets.

Compoz-A-Puzzle
1 Robert Lane
Glen Head, NY 11545-1444
800/343-5887
www.compozapuzzle.com
Makers of Puzzle Clonzz, intact, pre-cut, lightweight jigsaw puzzles that can be printed through a direct path printer.

Epson Store
P.O. Box 93107
Long Beach, CA 90809
800/873-7766
www.epsonstore.com
Banner paper, adhesive papers, cards, iron-on transfers, photo stickers, canvas paper, transparencies.

Invent-it
International Paper
Memphis, TN 38197
800/242-2148
www.invent-it.com
Greeting cards, banner paper, clear decals, stickers, iron-on transfers, poster paper, photo calendar kit.

JOBO Fototechnic
P.O. Box 3721
Ann Arbor, MI 48106
734/677-6989
www.jobo-usa.com
Makers of PhotoBryte Ink Jet products including photo paper, clear cling film, Kanvas Art Paper and transparency film.

Micro Format
830-3 Seton Court
Wheeling, IL 60090-5772
800/333-0549
www.paper-paper.com
Metallic paper, fabric carriers, quilting materials, transfer jigsaw puzzles, mouse pad kits, see-through window posters, glow-in-the-dark paper, dark shirt transfers and fuzzy paper as well as computer crafts kits and plastic craft materials (key rings, cups and so on).

Mirage Inkjet Technology
888/647-2436
www.mirageinkjet.com
A Premium Trial Pack includes samples of photo glossy paper, greeting card with envelope, transparency film, artist canvas, window decals, transfer paper and matte paper.

Paper Access
23 West 18th Street
New York, NY 10011
800/727-3701
www.paperaccess.com
Standard, recycled and exotic paper for computer printing and offset printing, including preprinted designs, metallics, vellums, labels, tent cards and stickers.

Paper Direct
P.O. Box 2970
Colorado Springs, CO 80901-2970
800/272-7377
www.paperdirect.com
Lettersheets, cards, brochures and postcards preprinted with color designs, ready to be printed with your message. A $25 PaperKit includes an assortment of paper samples plus tips and techniques.

Royal Brites
108 Main Street
Norwalk, CT 06851
800/526-4280
www.royalcrafts.com
The makers of Royal Lace paper doilies also make computer printable media including inkjet paper, magnet sheets, window decals, transparencies, transfers, fluorescent paper and vellum.

Xerox Corporation
Rochester, NY 14644
www.xerox.com
Inkjet magnet sheets, static cling window decals and a full line of other inkjet products.

Web Sites

General computer Information
FOLDOC (Free On-line Dictionary of Computing)
www.nightflight.com/foldoc/

Glossary of Computer Terms
www.ugeek.com/glossary/

Impresse Encyclopedia of Graphic Media
www.impresse.com
12,000 terms and 400 images on printing and graphic arts media terminology.

Magic in Red, Green and Blue
www.pagelab.com
A charming and informative series of short animations demonstrating how RGB color works. From the publisher of *Before & After* magazine.

Crafts
www.craftopia.com
Supplies for traditional arts and crafts plus project ideas and instructions.

www.creativejunctions.com
Home of the Craft and Hobby Search Ring.

www.zianet.com/mmlhess/craft.htm
Home of the Craft and Hobby Web Ring.

Paper
Co-op America's WoodWise Consumer Guide
www.woodwise.org
Practices, products and services that protect forests.

Digital Century
www.digitalcentury.com
Links to an article entitled "Printing: History and Development" which includes information on the history of paper.

Institute of Paper Science and Technology
www.ipst.edu
A graduate research center dedicated to the paper industry. Web site includes a virtual paper history library tour.

Save Hemp
www.savehemp.com
Site for contacting legislators with letters supporting hemp.

Art materials
www.nyu.edu/classes/miller/guide/
Links to "Drawing Materials and Drawing Techniques: A Guide and Glossary," a useful guide by NYU's Michael Miller.

Prepress and production
Adage Graphics Pre-Press Guides
Compiled by Doug Isaacs
www.adagegraphics.com
See the Tech Support section for downloadable PDF files that provide detailed information on preparing your files for output by a service bureau.

Typography
Adobe Type Foundry
www.adobe.com/type/main.html
Good information and tutorials on typography.

Counterspace
Dedicated to typography and its history
www.studiomotiv.com/counterspace
A beautiful and cleverly interactive Web site created by designer Brett Yancy Collins of Motivo design.

Font Site
www.fontsite.com
Magazine for type and graphics professionals.

Graphic design
Desktoppublishing.com
Information on using graphics software.

Museums
California Museum of Photography
University of California at Riverside
www.cmp.ucr.edu
Beautiful "virtual museum" design and exhibits of historical, contemporary and digital photography.

Book arts
Book Arts Web
www.philobiblion.com
Celebrates all the book arts with a gallery and links.

Nineteenth century print ephemera
Cigar Label Art
www.cigarlabelart.com
Hundreds of images, many printed in the 19th century. Includes a history of the chromolithography process.

Color Printing in the Nineteenth Century
www.lib.edel.edu/ud/spec/exhibits/color/index.html
Online version based on an exhibition at the University of Delaware in 1996.

History of American Greetings Company
www.americangreetings.com

Scrap Albums
www.scrapalbum.com
A delightful and beautifully designed online gallery from England of Victorian greeting cards, Valentines and scraps. Includes history and excellent links.

Government resources
Copyright Office
Library of Congress
Washington, DC 20559
www.cWeb.loc.gov/copyright/index.html

Stamps on-line
www.stamps.com
Service of the United States Postal Service allows on-line customers to buy, download and print postage stamps.

Organizations

Art safety
Center for Safety in the Arts
www.artswire.org:70/1/csa
The Center no longer has a physical address. Information on art safety is now listed on their Web site.

Book arts
The Center for Book Arts
28 West 27th Street, 3rd floor
New York, NY 10001
212/481-0295
www.centerforbookarts.org
Classes, exhibits, shows.

Minnesota Center for Book Arts
1011 Washington Ave. South, Suite 100
Minneapolis, MN 55415
612/338-3634
www.mnbookarts.org
Classes, exhibits, shows.

San Francisco Center for the Book
300 DeHaro Street
San Francisco, CA 94103
415/565-0545
www.sfcb.org
Classes, exhibits, shows.

Graphic and digital arts
American Institute of Graphic Arts
164 Fifth Avenue
New York, NY 10010
212/807-1990
www.aiga.org
This organization works to further excellence in the design industry.

Graphic Artists Guild
90 John Street, Suite 403
New York, New York 10038-3202
212/791-3400
www.gag.org
A national union of illustrators and designers. Publishes *The Graphic Artists Guild's Handbook of Pricing and Ethical Guidelines*.

International Association of Fine Arts Digital Printmakers
www.iafadp.org
A nonprofit organization founded in 1997 to encourage and support the development of the fine art digital print making industry; sponsors research on image permanence and new technologies.

Index

About the Author

JANET ASHFORD is a free-lance writer, artist and musician. Since 1989 she has written "how-to" articles on computer graphics for computer and design magazines including *Macworld, MacUser, Step-By-Step Electronic Design, Step-By-Step Graphics, Dynamic Graphics* and *Print*. Janet has created designs for books, newsletters and brochures and produced original illustrations for posters, textbooks, and magazines. She has taught summer classes in computer graphics at Kent State University and currently teaches regular classes in digital arts at the Mendocino Art Center in Mendocino, California.

Janet is the author or co-author of seven books on computer graphics and design, including:

- *The Arts and Crafts Computer: Using Your Computer as an Artist's Tool* (Peachpit Press, 2002)
- *Start with a Scan: A Guide to Transforming Scanned Photos and Objects into High Quality Art* with John Odam (2nd edition, Peachpit Press, 2000)
- *Getting Started with 3D: A Designer's Guide to 3D Graphics and Illustration* with John Odam (Peachpit Press, 1998)
- *Start with a Scan: A Guide to Transforming Scanned Photos and Objects into High Quality Art* with John Odam (1st edition, Peachpit Press, 1996)

- *Adobe Illustrator: A Visual Guide for the Mac* with Linnea Dayton (Graphic-Sha/Addison-Wesley, 1995)
- *Aldus PageMaker: A Visual Guide for the Mac* with Linnea Dayton (Graphic-Sha/Addison-Wesley, 1994)
- *The Verbum Book of PostScript Illustration* with Michael Gosney and Linnea Dayton (M&T Books, 1990)

Janet has worked as a fine artist for thirty years, creating drawings, paintings and posters with watercolor, acrylic, oil, pen-and-ink and silk screen. She is also a musician, composed and performed the original music for the interactive Photo CD that accompanies *The Official Photo CD Handbook* (Peachpit Press, 1995) and has composed a number of original Celtic-style jigs, reels and waltzes. She has performed and recorded early California music with Los Californios and Celtic music with Lime in the Harp, both based in San Diego, California. In Mendocino she performs regularly on violin with various folk music groups including The Fort Bragg Philharmonic (a duo), The Northern Troupe and The Bushwhackers Marching Band.

Before becoming involved with computer graphics, Janet lectured widely on the history of childbirth, wrote many books and articles on birth including *The Whole Birth Catalog* (Crossing Press, 1983) and *Birth Stories: The Experience Remembered* (Crossing Press, 1984) and for nine years published *Childbirth Alternatives Quarterly*. Her video *The Timeless Way: A History of Birth from Ancient to Modern Times* (InJoy Videos, 1998) was a winner of the 1999 National Educational Media Network Gold Apple Award.

Janet has a B.A. in psychology from the University of California at Los Angeles. She lives with her two daughters in Mendocino, California, on the coast about 120 miles north of San Francisco. Her web site is at www.jashford.com. You can contact her at 10377 Nichols Lane, Mendocino, CA 95460 or at jashford@jashford.com.